JOHANNA WALLIN

TRADITIONAL NORDIC KNITS

Over 40 Hats, Mittens, Gloves, and Socks

TRAFALGAR SQUARE
North Pomfret, Vermont

First published in the United States of America
in 2016 by
Trafalgar Square Books
North Pomfret, Vermont 05053

Published in Swedish by Norstedts as *Nordisk stickning*.

ISBN: 978-1-57076-770-8

Library of Congress Control Number: 2015952326

Thank you to Studio Norrgården in Vintrosa for contributing the beautiful mohair yarn that became the book's Damask pattern garments.

Interior Design: Gabriella Lindgren
Photography: Albin Dahlström
Photos of original mittens: Albin Dahlström, as well as Mona Lisa Djerf ©The Nordic Museum (page 39 Monogram, page 47 Small Blocks, page 103 Engagement Gloves), Haakon Harris/The Norwegian Folk Museum (page 69 Line Dance), Ritva Bäckman 1984/National Museum of Finland (page 87 Water Runner)
Landscape photos: ©Fotolia, as well as page 4 Patricia Rodas, pages 15, 16, 28, 96, 146 Albin Dahlström, page 152 Ulrika Korkala
Drawings: Johanna Wallin
Editor: Sophia Lundquist
Translator: Carol Huebscher Rhoades

Printed in China

10 9 8 7 6 5 4 3 2 1

TABLE OF CONTENTS

PREFACE

Winter in the Nordic countries is several months long, dark and cold—so there has always been a need for warm, close-fitting clothing. For that reason, knitting became an important handcraft early on. Mittens, hats, and socks were necessities for everyone, especially those working outside or in the army. Eventually these became commercial items and then status symbols throughout the region. The traditional Nordic star motif and the many small basic patterns were not only treats to the eye but contributed to making patterns tighter, thicker, and more durable. Many of these patterns became classics and continue to be timelessly attractive, particularly in an era when we look back longingly at the quality and longevity of classic handcrafts.

Nordic knitting patterns are more popular today than ever, but when did they originate, and from which areas? Sailors and merchants bought and sold knitted goods, and when new family bonds were forged, dowries in the form of knitted goods were exchanged between various parts of the region. I want to discuss some of these patterns and their likely origins in this book. Museums all over Scandinavia have preserved knitted items that can still dazzle us with their fantastic creativity and rich patterns. I've been inspired by these historic items, and have made modern pattern charts for hats, mittens, gloves, and socks from them so they can continue to survive for many more years. This is probably how patterns have always been developed and passed on: knitting a copy, trying to understand where the pattern fits into knitting tradition, and then showing someone else how to knit it, too.

Certain places have more distinguished pattern traditions than others, and luckily there are people who have worked extra hard to conserve that exceptional knitting heritage. One of those people is Hermanna Stengård, who worked as an elementary school teacher on the island of Gotland (in Sweden) at the beginning of the twentieth century. She was greatly interested in the knitting traditions of Gotland, and her students knitted garments with local motifs. She traveled around the island collecting patterns and garments for her book, *Gotland Knitting* (1925), and thanks to her, we know much more about Gotland knitting today than we would otherwise. Many of the items she preserved inspired the accessories in this book.

I hope to awaken your curiosity about textile history through this book, and perhaps inspire you to get out your family's knitted garments and see what history they have. I also hope you'll take a closer look at all the pattern treasuries around us in dresser drawers, old workboxes, and handcraft museums, before moths and overzealous cleaning destroy them.

Johanna

ABBREVIATIONS AND TECHNIQUES

This section explains the abbreviations in the instructions and describes some of the techniques used in this book. There are many different ways to do the same thing, so if you have a method you prefer to those listed here, use it. There is no right or wrong way, as long as the result is what you intended!

Abbreviations and terms

BO = bind off (= British cast off)

cm = centimeter(s)

CO = cast on

dbl dec = double decrease: sl 2 knitwise, k1, psso

dpn = double-pointed needles

in = inch(es)

k = knit

k2tog = k 2 together (= 1 st decreased; a right-leaning decrease)

k3tog = k 3 together: sl 1 knitwise, k2tog, psso (= 2 sts decreased)

LLI = left-lifted increase: k into left side of st below on right ndl

m = meter(s)

mm = millimeter(s)

ndl(s) = needle(s)

p = purl

p2tog = p 2 together (= 1 st decreased)

pm = place marker

psso = pass slipped stitch over

puk = pick up and knit

RLI = right-lifted increase: k into right side of st below 1st st on left ndl

rnd(s) = round(s)

RS = right side

sl = slip

slm = slip marker

ssk = sl, sl, k: (sl 1 knitwise) 2 times, insert left ndl tbl, k these 2 sts together (a left-leaning decrease)

Backward loop cast-on.

st(s) = stitch(es)

St st = stockinette st (= British stocking st)

tbl = through back loops

WS = wrong side

wyb = with yarn behind

wyf = with yarn forward

yd = yard(s)

yo = yarnover

- = instructions between * are repeated around or across. If the repeat isn't evenly divided over the round, there will be additional instructions before or after the asterisks which will be worked only once.

Double-pointed needles are numbered from the start of the round: Ndl 1 is the first needle with stitches on it, and Ndl 4 is the last.

CROCHET ABBREVIATIONS

ch = chain

dc = double crochet (= British treble crochet)

sc = single crochet (= British double crochet)

sl st = slip stitch

Techniques and tips

KNITTING TECHNIQUES

Garter stitch is worked by knitting on both the right and wrong sides. When you work two rows in garter stitch, a raised ridge appears on each side of the fabric. When you work garter stitch in the round, alternate rounds of knitting and rounds of purling to produce the same effect. See the garter stitch border on the Small Blocks pattern on page 40.

Stockinette is worked by knitting on the right side and purling on the wrong side. When you work stockinette in the round with the right side always facing you, knitting every round without any purl stitches to produce the same effect. See the single-color stockinette above the edging on the Damask pattern on page 70.

Two-color stranded knitting means that you work different stitches in different colors to form a pattern. The designs in this book have at most two colors in the same round, but two-color stranded knitting can also refer to designs with more than two colors per round.

It's easiest to work two-color stranded knitting in the round, since the right side is always visible.

While stitches are being worked with Color 1 of a two-color round, Color 2 lies or "floats" on the back of the work. If the floats are too long, they may catch on things. If there are more than five stitches between stitches of the same color, twist the two colors around each other on the wrong side to shorten the float.

There are many different ways to hold the yarns while working two-color stranded knitting: both strands over the left index finger, one strand over the left and one strand over the right, or one held at a time while the other hangs loose until needed. Use the method you're most comfortable with, but remember: It's important to hold the yarns the same way for the gauge swatch as for the actual garment knitting. The way you hold the yarn can affect both the gauge and the floats, and if you change methods, you might end up making uneven stripes. If you hold both yarns on one finger, you should make sure they're always in the same order— for example, the darker yarn always closer to your fingertip than the lighter yarn.

The stitches on the right side and floats on the wrong side make two-color stranded knitting thicker than single-color knitting. The fabric also draws in more. The gauge is often tighter in two-color stranded knitting, but different patterns draw in at different rates, so it's important to work your gauge swatch in the same pattern that will be used in the garment. If the garment will be knitted in the round, the gauge swatch should also be knitted in the round.

CHARTS

It's easiest to visualize a pattern if it's drawn up on a chart. The charts in this book are all set up to be read and worked from right to left, and from the bottom up. For garments knit in the round, all rounds begin at the right side of the chart. For garments knit in rows, begin right side rows at the right side of the chart and wrong side rows at the left side.

All charted rows show the design as seen from the right side. This means that if you're working a pattern in rows, stitches that appear as knit stitches on the chart must be purled on wrong side rows.

PATTERN REPEATS

A pattern repeat shows the smallest complete segment of stitches, rows, and colors in a pattern. You can calculate a pattern repeat by counting how many stitches there are until the pattern starts again. This includes both stitches and rows. Pattern repeats put together form the overall design.

Sometimes a pattern might be split by a larger repeat, as, for example, with the segments on the crown of a hat. If the hat has five segments that are all knitted alike, the chart will show one segment, which will then be worked five times total.

STITCH MARKERS

A stitch marker is a tool for keeping track of where you are in the pattern. Work to a marker, slip it to the other needle, and continue working on the other side. Some markers are as pretty as pieces of jewelry, but you can make your own markers by just tying a scrap piece of yarn into a loop.

To keep track of the number of rows between decreases or increases, it's a good idea to place a length of yarn between the stitches of the row where you work the decreases or increases. You can then count the number of rows above that yarn to see how many rows you've knitted since. The next time you decrease or increase, insert the yarn between the stitches of that row, and keep weaving it in and out as you go. When you're finished, just pull the loose yarn out.

FOLDLINES

If you're working in stockinette, a purl row or round on the right side becomes a foldline very readily.

You can also make a foldline by knitting a row or round on the right side with a needle one size larger than that used for the rest of the pattern. The resulting row is easy to fold.

JOINING THE CAST-ON EDGE OF A FACING

Work the desired number of rows or rounds in stockinette. Make a foldline with a purl row on the right side. Work the same number of rows or rounds after the foldline. Fold the piece at the foldline and join the live stitches to stitches picked up along the cast-on edge. Knit one live stitch together with one picked-up stitch around/across.

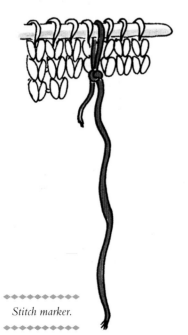

Stitch marker.

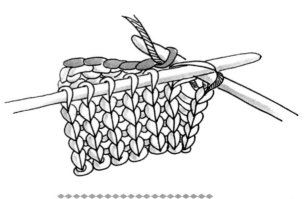

Joining the cast-on edge of a facing.

PICKING UP STITCHES FROM A CHAIN

Picking up stitches from a knitted surface and continuing can sometimes be easier if you crochet a chain first. Pick up new stitches either from both loops in the chain stitches or through the back loop only. Working through the back loop only makes a small visible edge that may help hide uneven edges. This method also makes it possible to ensure that the stitches are evenly distributed. For example, it's particularly useful for button bands along a sweater, or the edging on a hat.

WORKING IN THE OPPOSITE DIRECTION BY PICKING UP STITCHES FROM THE EDGE

When you make a thumb or a heel using a length of scrap yarn, the stitches picked up above the scrap yarn will be worked in the opposite direction from those picked up below. It's the same as if the piece had been turned upside down and the new stitches picked up from the lower edge.

When a knitted row is turned upside down, there's a shift of half a stitch in alignment. Because half-stitches can't be picked up, there will be one stitch less in the total. Therefore, you'll need to pick up one extra stitch to end up with the right number.

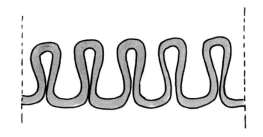

Stitch structure.

In stockinette, this won't be visible, but if you're ribbing from the opposite direction, there's a shift of half a stitch in alignment. It's not a mistake—it's just the structure of the stitches that makes this happen. As a comparison, think of a hand: there are five digits, but only four spaces separate those digits.

BINDING OFF (= BRITISH CASTING OFF)

Work one stitch and then another, and then pull the first over the second. Continue working one stitch and then pulling the previous stitch over it until all stitches have been bound off. Finish by cutting the yarn and drawing the end through the last stitch. If you work knit over knit and purl over purl, the bound-off edge will be extra stretchy.

Picking up stitches from a chain.

Binding off.

Mittens and Gloves

THUMBS WITH SCRAP YARN

A thumb formed using scrap yarn is best for a wider, heavier mitten that won't be tightly stretched over the palm. If the range of motion proves to be too small, the mitten will start to twist diagonally over the hand.

Use a length of smooth, contrast-color scrap yarn long enough to knit the thumbhole stitches with a bit to spare.

Leave the pattern yarn hanging and knit the thumbhole stitches with the scrap yarn. If there are still stitches on the needle, slip them and switch back to the pattern yarn. Knit the scrap yarn stitches with the pattern yarn, and then continue with the rest of the mitten.

Then knit the thumb: Pick up the stitches below the scrap yarn, and then an equal number above. Remove the scrap yarn a stitch at a time.

THUMBS WITH GUSSETS

A mitten with a thumb gusset allows ample movement by the thumb. To help keep track of the stitches for the gusset, place markers between the gusset stitches and the rest of the hand.

A **symmetric gusset** has increases on each side of the stitches at the base of the gusset. When

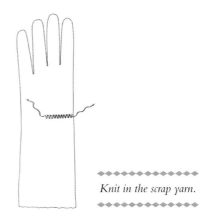

Knit in the scrap yarn.

the gusset is the desired width, put the gusset stitches on a holder. Cast on the same number of stitches as replacements.

A **single-sided gusset** only has increases on the outer edge and is a combination of a symmetric gusset and the scrap-yarn method. This style works well for patterned mittens, since the motifs won't be broken up by increases.

Increase on every other round. The total number of stitches needed depends on the length of the gusset. The remaining stitches needed for the thumb are "borrowed" by casting on new stitches at the thumbhole, as for a symmetric gusset. Place the gusset stitches and the "borrowed" stitches on holders, and then cast on the same number of stitches as replacements.

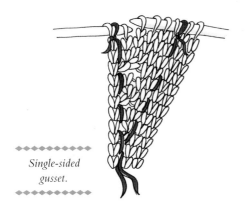

Single-sided gusset.

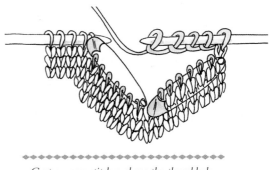

Cast on new stitches above the thumbhole.

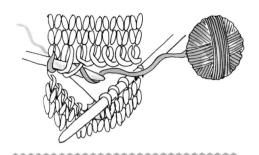

Pick up and knit new stitches above the thumbhole.

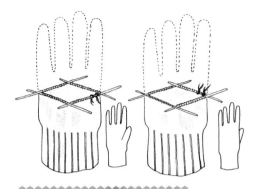

Placement of thumb on gloves.

Begin the thumb by picking up new stitches in the backward loop cast-on (which were the new stitches for the thumbhole) and then slip the held stitches back onto the needles.

GLOVE FINGERS

It's important to place glove fingers correctly in relation to the thumb so the thumb doesn't suddenly end up next to the little finger. Always double-check before you start knitting fingers.

If you knit the right thumb at the start of the round and the left thumb at the end of the round, they'll be placed so you can make the fingers at the same spots on both gloves.

When you've knitted the glove up to the base of the little finger, divide the stitches for the fingers.

Place the stitches for the little finger on a holder (safety pins work well for this) and cast on new stitches between the little and ring fingers. Knit 2-4 rounds in stockinette with the remaining stitches (including the newly cast-on stitches). The glove will fit better with the little finger seated a bit lower on the hand than the rest.

To ensure that each of the fingers is wide enough and fits well in relation to your hand, cast on new stitches between each pair of fingers.

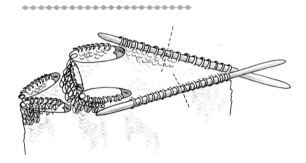

Dividing the stitches for the fingers.

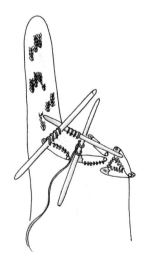

Cast on and pick up and knit stitches between the fingers.

Socks and stockings

HEELS WITH SCRAP YARN

Half of a sock's stitches are used for the heel. If the sock is 64 stitches around, knit 32 stitches in scrap yarn to mark them off.

Work the sock to the beginning of the heel.

Use a length of smooth, contrast-color scrap yarn long enough to knit the heel stitches with a bit to spare.

Leave the pattern yarn hanging and knit the heel stitches with the scrap yarn. Slide the scrap yarn stitches back to the left needle, switch to the pattern yarn, and knit them again.

Knit the heel: Pick up the stitches below the scrap yarn, and then an equal number above.

Remove the scrap yarn a stitch at a time. Sometimes it's easier to remove the scrap yarn if you cut it into shorter sections—but be careful not to cut the pattern yarn. Knit the heel in the round, decreasing as for the toe; don't decrease on the first round.

HEELS WITH HEEL FLAPS

Place the instep stitches on a holder and work the heel flap back and forth.

When the heel flap is long enough, shape it with short rows and then pick up and knit new stitches on each side of the flap. Make sure you pick up and knit stitches the same way on each side so the heel will be nice and even.

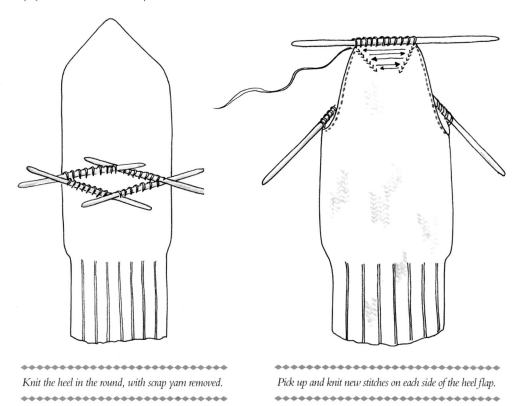

Knit the heel in the round, with scrap yarn removed.

Pick up and knit new stitches on each side of the heel flap.

Tassels, pompoms, and I-cords

There are many ways to embellish a hat. Tassels and pompoms can be made in a variety of sizes, and can also be used to decorate mittens and socks.

TASSELS

Measure the desired length of the tassel and add ½ in / 1 cm so you can trim it until it's even. Wrap enough yarn for your desired tassel thickness around a piece of cardboard or something else sturdy.

Tassel.

Cut one end of the wound yarn open and lay it flat.

Wrap a short length of a matching or nicely contrasting yarn a couple times around the center of the yarn bundle, and then fold the tassel and wrap a few more times to secure. Knot the wrapping yarn well and then cut it. Use a tapestry needle to weave the ends into the middle of the tassel.

Knit an I-cord and sew the tassel to it; then sew the cord to the garment.

Pompom.

POMPOMS

Draw two circles of the same size on a piece of cardboard, with smaller circles at their centers. The distance between the inner circle and the outer circle will be the length of the yarn from the pompom's center out.

Cut out the outer circles and cut away the inner ones. Align them and wrap yarn around them so that it passes through the inner circles. It's easier to wrap the yarn if it's threaded onto a tapestry needle—and you can thread more than one strand on to speed things up. Wrap until no more yarn will fit through the center holes.

Insert the scissor tips between the circles and cut around. Pull the circles apart just far enough to let you wrap some very strong thread around the yarn between the circles. Tie firmly and trim ½ in / 1 cm from the knot.

Remove the cardboard circles and trim the pompom if necessary. If the pompom's made with wool yarn, you can stick a fork in it and hold it over steaming water to fluff it up—but be careful not to scald yourself.

Sew the pompom to the garment with a few stitches at the center. Trim the ends so they don't show.

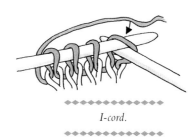

I-cord.

I-CORDS

An I-cord can be knitted with 2, 3, 4, or 5 stitches. More makes it difficult to keep the cord even. Use double-pointed needles; cast on stitch number and knit. Do not turn. Instead, slide the stitches back to the tip of the needle and knit another row on the right side. Tug the yarn after the first stitch to close the gap. When the I-cord is the desired length, cut yarn, draw the end through, and secure it inside the cord with back stitch.

WOOL AND YARN

There are so many beautiful yarns to choose from—
maybe you even spin your own! Wool's excellent
qualities are found not only in sheep's wool but
also in alpaca and angora mohair.

In earlier times, sheep's wool was the most common fiber used for yarn in the Nordic countries. Almost every household kept sheep, and spinning was a task every woman learned to do as a child. It was a necessity then, but now most people spin as a relaxing and enjoyable hobby. Handspun yarns will work well for the patterns in this book—as long as the gauge is correct.

One of the most important requirements for a satisfying knitting project is the right yarn. Today you have many lovely yarns meant for a variety of purposes to choose between—back when many of this book's original garments were knitted, the only choice would have been what came from the household sheep. To make the best choice, it's important to consider the type of wool, its preparation, and the way the yarn was spun. Knowledge of traditional methods can help you when you are choosing yarn for your projects.

First, decide what kind of wool will be best for your project. Lambs' wool is the softest; as sheep age, their wool becomes coarser, and rams tend to have the coarsest wool. Rams' wool, with a little natural lanolin left in, makes excellent work mittens for winter—lambs' wool is just right for making a soft baby sweater. If you swap the wool choices for these garments, the recipient will probably be disappointed!

If you want to spin your own yarn, the time of year when the sheep was sheared is also important. Wool shorn in fall, after the ewes have been outside eating well all summer, is finer than wool shorn in spring, when the sheep have been inside for months and any lambs already born have taken a lot of nourishment and energy from their mothers.

The wool quality will also differ depending on what part of the body it comes from. Wool on the shoulders and sides is finest and most lustrous. Commercial yarn usually has no information on this—industrially-spun yarns blend various types of wool for high overall quality.

Even the sheep breed can be important: The wool of some breeds has finer fibers and thus will lend itself particularly well to some projects.

When wool feels prickly, it's because the fiber used in that particular yarn is so thick that it doesn't bend easily when it touches the skin, and the skin feels the fiber poking it. If the fiber is thin enough to bend on contact with skin, it won't be felt nearly as much. Therefore, it's important to keep the fineness of the wool in mind if you want a really soft yarn, rather than judging the yarn solely by how fluffy it feels in your hand. A loosely-spun yarn can feel soft when you touch it with your fingers but still contain coarse fibers.

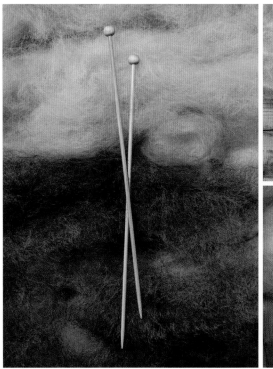

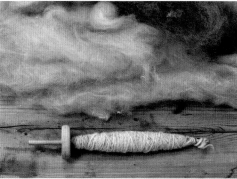

It's easy to felt wool—everyone's had the experience, at one point or another, of putting a wool garment into water that's too hot, and taking out a garment that's both smaller and more compact than it used to be. At those moments, wool's felting ability doesn't seem so great; but if you want a pair of mittens that resist moisture and are extremely durable, it's quite useful. To control the degree of felting, I recommend you felt by hand. If you're felting mittens, put them on your hands and rub them with warm water and wool-safe soap or shampoo. Knitted stitches with be set slightly by felting, which makes the fabric strong.

Besides wool, there are many other natural fibers from both plants and animals that are an excellent choice for yarn. In this book, wool was primarily used, but yarn of other fiber types is occasionally recommended.

Alpaca wool is a soft, flexible, and fine fiber that comes from a camel relative, the alpaca. The fiber is often long and somewhat more lustrous than sheep's wool, which makes for a pretty fleece. And that lovely fleece is something to long for if you're making a lace shawl—but if your plan is a sturdy pattern-knitted tam, the tam will be slouchy if you make it with alpaca wool, no matter how well it was knitted. For good pattern knitting with alpaca wool, the yarn needs to be loosely spun and tightly knitted so that the pattern will show. Blending sheep and alpaca wool makes a soft, strong yarn that suits the patterns in this book.

Mohair is what the fiber from an Angora goat is called. White mohair is whiter than white sheep's wool, and doesn't yellow as easily. The fibers are long and shiny, with a pretty luster. Mohair is excellent for knitting structured stitch patterns and makes lovely, durable stockings if firmly knitted.

Cotton was first imported into Scandinavia in the early 1700s. Because there was no other way to get it, it was considered a luxury fiber and used very sparingly. Cotton is a plant fiber with a whiteness seldom found in wool. As a result it was often used as a pattern color. You can blend wool and cotton as long as the garment is washed with the care required for the more sensitive fiber—which, in this case, would be the wool.

Sock yarn is its own separate category, usually a blend of wool and a synthetic fiber—normally about 75% wool and 25% nylon or polyester. There are many high-quality sock yarns on the market, and the synthetic blends make socks more durable. It's always disappointing to knit pretty socks that only last for a few outings. Most of these yarns are superwash-treated and can be machine washed.

Substituting yarns

All the garments in this book are knitted more firmly than the gauge given on the yarn ball band. That makes the items stronger and helps them hold their shape better.

You can substitute your favorite yarns for those suggested, or spin your own yarn if you prefer. Here are some tips for substituting yarns.

GAUGE

Every pattern lists the gauge for the garment. A suggested needle size is also listed, but the actual needle size that will achieve the gauge may vary from person to person.

To determine what size needles to use, you must knit a gauge swatch—widely considered the least popular part of planning a new knitting project. Consider the gauge swatch a form of insurance: It'll be even less enjoyable for you if the garment you took so much time and trouble to make doesn't fit. The gauge swatch is also a way to make sure you like the pattern and colors. If you're sick of them by the time you finish the gauge swatch, it's unlikely you'll ever finish the whole pattern.

If you want to knit a pattern you've designed, you'll need to knit a gauge swatch to determine the number of stitches and rows in various parts of the garment. If you're knitting a published pattern, you'll need the gauge swatch to ensure the size is correct.

Your swatch may not match the gauge given in in the instructions, even if you're using the suggested yarn and needle size—we all knit at different tensions. If your swatch is too loose (i.e., you have fewer stitches and rows than you should), try needles that are a size smaller. If your swatch is too tight (i.e., you have more stitches and rows than you should), try needles that are a size larger.

If the garment will be knitted in the round in two-color stranded knitting, knit the gauge swatch the same way. You can cut the swatch open afterward to lay it flat for measuring.

Finishing the gauge swatch is an important part of the process. When knitted fabric is washed, it smooths out; the stitches even out and stretch slightly.

Do not make your gauge swatch too small. Ideally, it should be 4¼ x 4¼ in / 11 x 11 cm, but 2½ x 2½ in / 6 x 6 cm will work at a minimum.

Use an old postcard or piece of cardboard and cut out a square hole, 4 x 4 in / 10 x 10 cm or 2 x 2 in / 5 x 5 cm. Place the hole over the knitting and count the number of stitches and the number of rows. For the smaller hole, double the numbers of rows and stitches you have to approximate a gauge of 4 x 4 in / 10 x 10 cm. Now you can use these numbers to determine the measurements per inch / cm. For example, 32 stitches x 40 rows = 4 x 4 in / 10 x 10 cm is the same as 8 sts x 10 rows = 1 inch / 3.2 stitches x 4 rows = 1 x 1 cm. It's better to begin by measuring the stitch and row count in 4 in / 10 cm and then divide the numbers by 4 / 10 for the stitches and rows per inch or centimeter than to try to measure individual stitches or rows—it's difficult to measure partial stitches or rows, but it is important for garment fit.

YARN THICKNESS

Measuring the thickness of yarn is rather imprecise because it depends on how hard the yarn has been spun. High twist yarn is thinner than loosely spun yarn even when the length and weight are the same. Even the fiber type can influence the yarn thickness. For example, alpaca is a thicker fiber than Merino wool.

Industrially spun yarn usually lists the number of yards and/or meters per 100 g, such as 382 yd/350 m / 100 g.

Sometimes you might also see the metric value as "No." which stands for the number of meters per gram of single-ply yarn. Yarn labeled as No. 7/2 consists of two strands of yarn that are each 7 m/g. When two such strands are plied together, the finished yarn is 3.5 m/g, which is the same as 350 m per 100 g.

To simplify comparing different yarns, you can use the wraps per inch (WPI) as a metric. When the WPI is taken into consideration with the yardage or meterage, you can make a fairly good comparison between yarns.

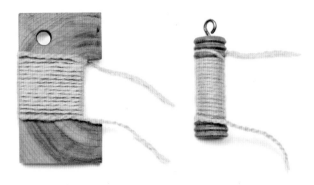

WPI measures. Wind the yarn around and count the number of wraps that fit to figure out the WPI.

Wrap the yarn around a ruler or a WPI measure and count the number of wraps of yarn that will fit side by side in one inch / 2.54 cm. Wrap tightly enough that the strands cozy up next to each other, but do not press them into each other. This method works very well for handspun yarn, which usually does not have a given number of yards/meters / 100 g.

If the yarn you want to use is only a little thicker or thinner than the suggested yarn, you might try knitting it with larger needles for a thinner yarn or thinner needles for a heavier yarn. Keep in mind that somewhat loosely knitted fabric is more flexible than knitting that is too firm.

Make a gauge swatch and compare for the best results!

Yarns and substitute yarns for the patterns in this book

This chart lists the yarns used in the book as well as yarns that were test-knitted as alternates. There are many other fine yarns you can use. Compare these with your own favorites and knit your own test swatches.

LACE YARN (CYCA #0, LIGHT FINGERING)

Name	Producer	yd/m / 100g	Fiber Content	WPI
Røros lamullgarn	Rauma	546/500	100% lambs' wool	20
Tynd uld	Geilsk	628/575	100% wool	21
Duo	Design Club DK	590/540	100% wool	21
Tvinni	Isager	560/512	100% Merino wool	22
Spindrift	Jamieson's of Shetland	459/420	100% Shetland wool	20

SUPER-FINE YARN (CYCA #1, FINGERING/BABY)

Name	Producer	yd/m / 100g	Fiber Content	WPI
Gårdens mohairgarn 2-ply	Ateljé Norrgården	393/360	100% mohair	18
Finullgarn	Rauma	382/350	100% wool	18
Elegance	Blacker Yarns	382/350	80% wool, 20% alpaca	16
Shetland 4-ply	Blacker Yarns	382/350	100% wool	15
Classic 4-ply	Blacker Yarns	382/350	100% wool	16
Welsh Mountain 4-ply	Blacker Yarns	382/350	100% wool	16

FINE YARN (CYCA #2, SPORT/BABY)

Name	Producer	yd/m / 100g	Fiber Content	WPI
Visjögarn	Östergötlands ullspinneri	328/300	100% wool	16
Gammelserie	Rauma	349/320	100% wool	16
Double knitting	Jamieson's of Shetland	328/300	100% wool	16

SOCK YARN (CYCA #1)

Name	Producer	yd/m / 100g	Fiber Content	WPI
Jawoll	Lang Yarns	459/420	75% wool, 25% polyamide	21
Regia	Schachenmayr	459/420	75% wool, 25% polyamide	20
Fabel	Drops	448/410	75% wool, 25% polyamide	21
British Wool & Mohair	Blacker Yarns	485/444	90% mohair, 10% nylon	20

COTTON YARN (CYCA #1)

Name	Producer	yd/m / 100g	Fiber Content	WPI
Pimabomuld	CaMaRose	437/400	100% cotton	24
Mandarin petit	Sandnes garn	393/360	100% cotton	22

HOURGLASS

Mittens and hat

This mitten–and–hat set will be easy to knit. With small adjustments in the pattern repeat, you can change the sizing or work with different yarn. To best show off the pattern effect, choose two colors that contrast strongly.

FINISHED MEASUREMENTS

Mittens: total length 11½ in / 29 cm; thumbhole to mitten tip 6¼ in / 16 cm; hand circumference 8 in / 20.5 cm.
Hat: circumference 21½ in / 54 cm; length 9 in / 23 cm.

YARN

CYCA #1 (fingering/baby) Blacker Black Welsh Mountain 4-ply (190 yd/174 m / 50 g; 16 WPI), black.
CYCA #1 (fingering/baby) Blacker Classic 4-ply (190 yd/174 m / 50 g; 16 WPI), white.
Substitute yarns: Rauma Finullgarn, Östergötland Visjögarn, Blacker Elegance or any yarn which knits to the same gauge.

YARN AMOUNTS

Mittens: Color 1 (Black), 50g; Color 2 (White), 50g.
Hat: Color 1 (Black), 50g; Color 2 (White), 50g; for the tassel, Color 1 (black), 10g.

NOTIONS

Smooth contrast-color scrap yarn.

NEEDLES

U.S. size 1-2 / 2.5 mm: 16 in / 40 cm circular and set of 5 dpn.

GAUGE

31 sts and 30 rnds in pattern = 4 x 4 in / 10 x 10 cm (wet-blocked swatch).
Adjust needle size to obtain correct gauge if necessary.

Pattern repeat = 8 sts and 8 rows.

Please read instructions completely before beginning to knit.

HOURGLASS
Mittens

The hourglass motif on the original mitten is 10 sts x 10 rows. By reducing the block to 8 sts x 8 rows, the mitten will have the same number of repeats around as the original even though it's knitted with heavier yarn. If you want to knit with even heavier yarn, use the larger pattern repeat but work fewer repeats around. There are many ways to arrange this little pattern motif.

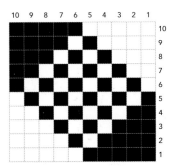

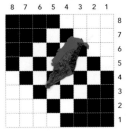

The small hourglass repeat can easily be adjusted for different sizes.

With Color 1 and dpn, CO 56 sts. Divide sts onto dpn and join. Work 10 rnds in St st.

Purl 1 rnd (= foldline).

Work in pattern, following chart for mitten. After increases in Row 1 of chart, there will be 64 sts around.

The chart only shows half of mitten; knit other side the same way, except for thumbhole.

Work Rows 9–16 4 times.

THUMB PLACEMENT Place right thumbhole by knitting first 16 sts on Ndl 1 with scrap yarn (green line on chart).

For left thumb, knit last 16 sts on Ndl 2 (red line on chart). Slide thumbhole sts back onto left ndl and work in pattern.

Repeat Rows 17–24 4 times (adjust number of repeats for a longer or shorter mitten if desired).

Shape top of mitten, following Rows 25–40 of chart. Cut yarn and draw end through rem sts.

THUMB Puk 16 sts below scrap yarn and 16 sts above; carefully remove scrap yarn. Divide sts onto 3 dpn.

Work the 32 thumb sts, following Rows 9–16 of chart 2 times + Row 17 (or to desired length).

Shape top of thumb, following Rows 34–40 of chart.

Cut yarn and draw end through rem sts.

Fold cuff facing to WS and sew down securely.

Make other mitten the same way, placing thumb correctly.

Weave in all ends neatly on WS. Wash mittens in lukewarm water with wool-safe soap. Rinse if necessary. Roll in towel and then lay flat to dry.

	knit on RS, purl on WS with Color 2
■	knit on RS, purl on WS with Color 1
◣	ssk with Color 1
◿	k2tog with Color 2
Ω	backward loop CO with Color 2

Half of mitten. The red line marks left thumb placement and the green line marks right thumb placement.

HOURGLASS
Hat

With Color 1 and short circular, CO 140 sts. Join, being careful not to twist cast-on row. Pm for beg of rnd. Work 10 rnds in St st.

Purl 1 rnd (= foldline).

Work in pattern, following the chart for the hat. After the increases in Row 1, there will be 160 sts around.

The chart only shows a fourth of the hat; knit the other three sections the same way.

Work Rows 9–16 4 times.

Tip: Pm at each of the 8 decrease lines; use a different color/type of stitch marker to denote beginning of rnd.

Work the crown shaping, following the chart. When sts no longer fit around circular, change to dpn.

Cut yarn and draw end through rem sts.

Weave in all ends neatly on WS. Wash the hat in lukewarm water with wool-safe soap. Rinse if necessary. Roll in towel and then place over an inflated balloon (size equivalent to head of wearer) to dry.

TASSEL With Color 1 and dpn, knit an I-cord with 4 sts and 60 rows. Make a tassel with Color 1 and sew securely to the end of the I-cord. Sew the other end of the I-cord securely to the tip of the hat. For more details, see "Tassels, pompoms, and I-cords" on page 13.

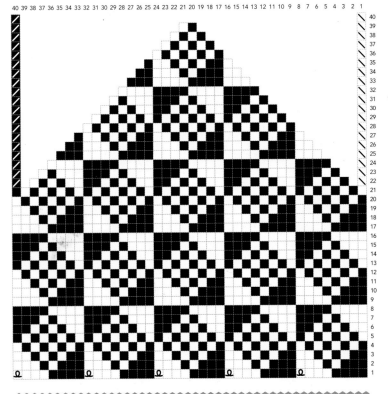

	knit on RS, purl on WS with Color 2
	knit on RS, purl on WS with Color 1
\\	ssk with Color 2
/	k2tog with Color 1
Ω	backward loop CO with Color 2

A fourth of the hat. Knit the other three sections the same way.

*The hat in this photo is half a pattern repeat longer than shown in
the chart. This shows how easy it is to adjust the sizing.*

HOURGLASS
Original pattern

It's amazing that these well-used mittens were preserved as a pair. They were knitted with handspun wool and, thanks to the color changes, we can tell that the left mitten was knitted before the right one. When the knitter ran out of the brown yarn, she or he just started using another skein. Maybe the difference in color was not as apparent then, but over time the different yarns have faded differently. The thumbs were knitted last of all—they both also use that same lighter color of yarn.

These were everyday mittens, and even if the yarn was spliced, they were pattern-knitted for warmth and durability. The careful

mending also speaks of thrift and the high value put on knitted garments.

Seeing the sequence of work in these mittens makes us feel closer to the person who knitted them so long ago. These mittens are some of the knitted garments that Hermanna Stengård collected at the beginning of the 1920s, but they were in use many years before then.

Today these mittens are preserved in the collection of the
Gotland County Handicraft Association in Visby.

MONOGRAM

Mittens and socks

You can add the year and your initials to these
mittens and socks, as I did. Keep in mind that the
initials and numbers must be knitted upside down
on the sock legs in order to make them right side
up when the socks are worn.

FINISHED MEASUREMENTS
Mittens: total length 10¾ in / 27 cm;
thumbhole to mitten tip 5¼ in / 13.5 cm; hand
circumference 7½ in / 19 cm.
Socks: leg length 5½ in / 14 cm; foot length 9
in / 23 cm; foot circumference 8¾ in / 22 cm.

YARN
Mittens: CYCA #0 (lace/light fingering) Rauma
Røros lamb's wool (Lamullgarn) (273 yd/250 m /
50 g; 20 WPI).
Socks: CYCA #1 (sock) Lang Jawoll (230 yd/210
m / 50 g; 21 WPI).
Substitute mitten yarn: Jamieson Spindrift or
any yarn that knits to the same gauge.
Substitute sock yarn: Schachenmayr Regia, Drops
Fabel, or any yarn that knits to the same gauge.

YARN AMOUNTS
Mittens: Color 1 (Black), 50 g; Color 2 (Red), 50 g.
Socks: Color 1 (Black), 50 g; Color 2 (Red), 50 g.

NOTIONS
2 large safety pins or stitch holders; smooth
contrast-color scrap yarn.

NEEDLES
U.S. size 0 / 2 mm: set of 4 or 5 dpn

GAUGE
Mittens: 38 sts and 38 rnds in pattern = 4 x 4
in / 10 x 10 cm (wet-blocked swatch).
Socks: 38 sts and 38 rnds in pattern = 4 x 4 in /
10 x 10 cm (wet-blocked swatch).
Adjust needle size to obtain correct gauge if
necessary.

Pattern repeat, basic motif = 4 sts and 6 rows.

Please read instructions completely before
beginning to knit.

MONOGRAM
Mittens

Add your own initials and the year using the alphabet and numbers from Gerda's sampler (page 38).

With Color 2 and dpn, CO 72 sts. Divide sts onto dpn and join. Work 10 rnds in St st.

Purl 1 rnd (= foldline).

Work right mitten following chart for right mitten, and left mitten following chart for left mitten (pages 34-35).

THUMB GUSSET Begin thumb gusset with 1 st from hand: on right mitten, begin with the st between the 3rd and 5th sts of Rows 23–53. Work gusset, following Rows 1–31 of chart on page 33.

Place left thumb between the 67th and 69th sts, Rows 23–53. Work gusset following Rows 1–31 of chart on page 33.

Tip: Pm at outer st on each side of gusset and work gusset between markers.

On Row 54 of mitten, place the 31 sts of thumb gusset onto 2 safety pins or a holder, as indicated on the charts for the right/left mitten. CO 1 st with a backward loop over the gap and then continue following charted pattern.

Repeat Rows 56–61 5 times (if you want a longer or shorter mitten, work repeat more or fewer times).

Right mitten with symmetric thumb gusset.

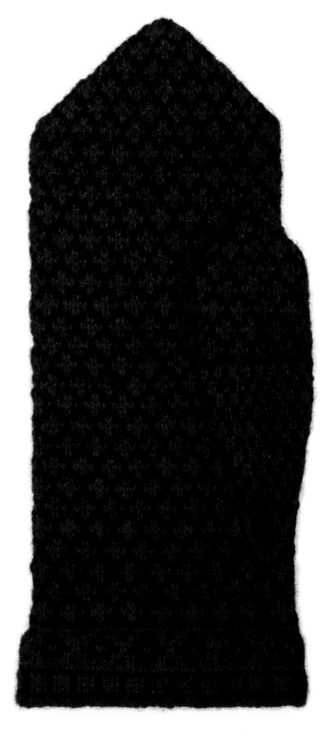

After completing charted rows and top shaping, cut yarn and draw end through rem 8 sts.

THUMB Puk 1 st in the backward loop cast on over thumbhole. Slide the 31 gusset sts to a needle and then divide these 32 sts onto 3 dpn.

The round for the thumb begins at the st picked up in the cast-on loop of thumbhole.

Work following Rows 32–55 of the thumb chart.

The thumb can be lengthened or shortened as desired.

After completing last rnd, cut yarn and draw through rem sts.

Fold the cuff facing to the WS and sew down securely.

Make the other mitten the same way, placing thumb correctly.

Weave in all ends neatly on WS. Wash mittens in lukewarm water with wool-safe soap. Rinse if necessary. Roll in towel and then lay flat to dry.

Thumb gusset and thumb.

- ■ knit on RS, purl on WS with Color 2
- ■ knit on RS, purl on WS with Color 1
- ▲ double decrease with Color 1
- ⌒ yarnover with Color 2
- 🎀 k1tbl into yarnover with Color 2
- 0 puk 1 st with Color 1

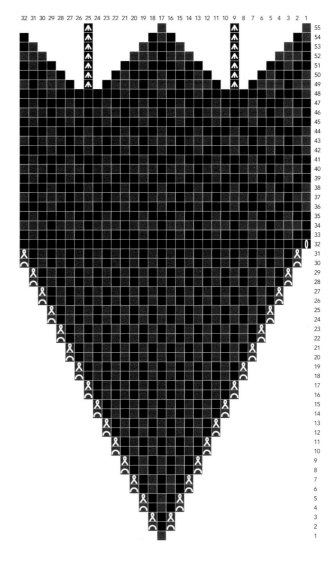

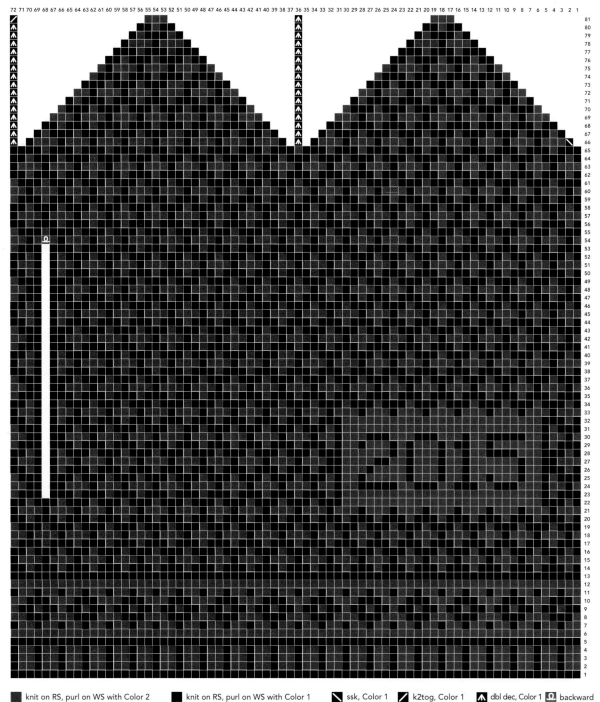

Left mitten.

knit on RS, purl on WS with Color 2 ■ knit on RS, purl on WS with Color 1 ◣ ssk, Color 1 ◢ k2tog, Color 1 ▲ dbl dec, Color 1 Ω backward loop CO, Color 2

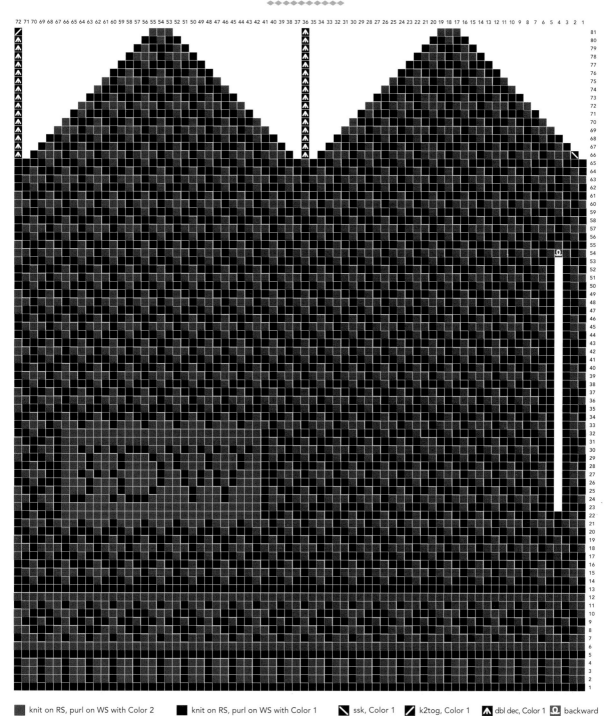

knit on RS, purl on WS with Color 2   knit on RS, purl on WS with Color 1   ◣ ssk, Color 1   ◢ k2tog, Color 1   ⋀ dbl dec, Color 1   Ω backward loop CO, Color 2

MONOGRAM
Socks

Add your own initials and year. Keep in mind that initials and numbers must be knitted upside down on sock legs to be the right side up when socks are worn.

With Color 2 and dpn, CO 84 sts. Divide sts onto dpn and join. Knit 10 rnds in St st.

Purl 1 rnd (= foldline).

Knit right and left socks following the chart, noting where heel is placed on each so block with initials and year will be on outside of each sock and row changes will be on the inside.

Work Rows 35–40 2 times.

Left sock: Work heel over sts 43-84 with scrap yarn (green line on chart). Slide sts back to left ndl and knit in pattern.

Right sock: Work heel over sts 1-42 with scrap yarn (white line on chart). Slide sts back to left ndl and knit in pattern.

Work foot, following chart. Repeat Rows 44–49 8 times (if you want a longer or shorter sock, work repeat more or fewer times).

Cut yarn and draw end through rem sts.

HEEL Pick up 42 sts below scrap yarn at heel and 42 sts above. Carefully remove scrap yarn.

Increase 1 st at each side and work following the heel chart. The rnd begins at center of sole.

The chart only shows half of heel; work other half the same way.

After completing the heel, cut yarn and draw end through rem sts. Fold facing at top of sock under

and sew down on WS.

Make second sock the same way, placing heel correctly.

Weave in all ends neatly on WS. Wash socks in lukewarm water with wool-safe soap. Rinse if necessary. Roll in towel and then lay flat to dry.

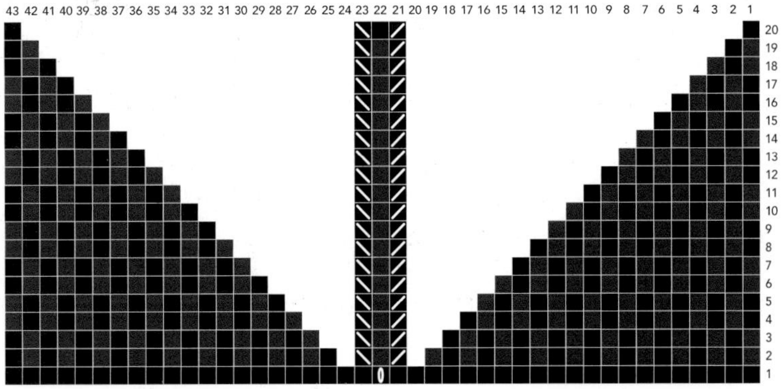

Sock with year.

Half of heel. Knit other half the same way. Rnd begins at center of sole.

■ knit on RS, purl on WS with Color 2
■ knit on RS, purl on WS with Color 1
�◣ ssk with Color 1
◢ k2tog with Color 1
0 puk 1 st with Color 1

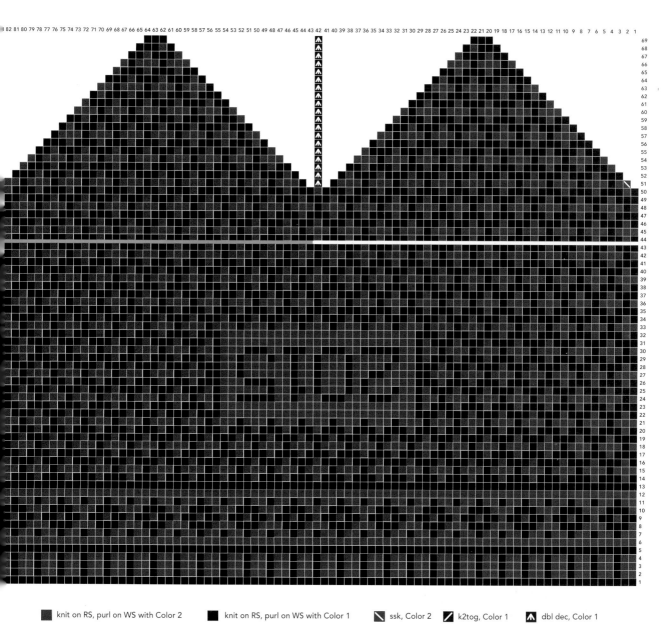

knit on RS, purl on WS with Color 2 knit on RS, purl on WS with Color 1 ssk, Color 2 k2tog, Color 1 dbl dec, Color 1

Add your own initials and the year to the pattern using the alphabet and numbers from Gerda's sampler.

The letters and numbers can also be used for other garments. If you have a larger surface to fill, you can make the text larger or longer. For example, whole stories have been knitted into garments or embroidered on other textiles.

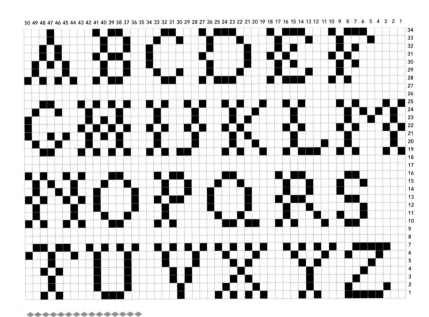

Alphabet, lowercase.

Alphabet, uppercase.

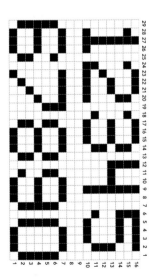

Numbers.

MONOGRAM
Original pattern

This beautiful sampler was embroidered in 1888 by my great-grandmother, Gerda. It is sewn on burlap, which is a simple fabric for a little crofter girl to sew on. Over time, Gerda became an expert seamstress and the sampler has inspired several generations. You can see from the flags on the sampler that Norway and Sweden were united at that time.

It used to be common to mark one's clothing, knitted or sewn, with initials and the year. Usually the monogram had three initials: The first letter stood for the person's first name, the second for the first letter of the father's first name, and the third letter was D for "daughter" or S for "son". Today it is more typical to use the initials of first and last names, and sometimes the middle initial.

The original mittens can be found in the Nordic Museum in Stockholm. They were purchased in 1901 and came from the parish of Ullared in Halland.

SMALL BLOCKS

Mittens, socks, and hat

This set features a truly classic motif. It's easy to knit even for those inexperienced with two-color stranded knitting because there aren't long floats between the colors. It's also easy to remember the pattern repeat, which is simple with just two colors. This motif looks just as nice in a light color against a dark background.

FINISHED MEASUREMENTS

Mittens: total length 10¼ in / 26 cm; thumbhole to tip 5 in / 13 cm; hand circumference 7 in / 18 cm.
Socks: leg length 5¼ in / 13 cm; foot length 9½ in / 24 cm; foot circumference 8 in / 20 cm.
Hat: circumference 21¼ in / 54 cm; length 8¾ in / 22 cm.

YARN

Mittens and hat: CYCA #2 (sport/baby) Östergötland Visjögarn (328 yd/300 m / 100 g; 16 WPI).
Socks: CYCA #1 (sock) Drops Fabel (224 yd/205 m / 50 g; 21 WPI).
Substitute mitten and hat yarn: Rauma Finullgarn or Gammelserie, Blacker Elegance, or any yarn that knits to the same gauge.
Substitute sock yarn: Schachenmayr Regia or any yarn that knits to the same gauge.

YARN AMOUNTS

Mittens: Color 1 (White), 50g; Color 2 (Gray), 50g.
Socks: Color 1 (White), 50g; Color 2 (Gray), 50g.

Hat: Color 1 (White), 40g; Color 2 (Gray), 40g; for the tassel, Color 2 (Gray), 10g.

NOTIONS

2 large safety pins or stitch holders; smooth contrast-color scrap yarn.

NEEDLES

U.S. size 1-2 / 2.5 mm: set of 5 dpn and 16 in / 40 cm circular.

GAUGE

Mittens and hat: 31 sts and 32 rnds in pattern = 4 x 4 in / 10 x 10 cm (wet-blocked swatch).
Socks: 32 sts and 34 rnds in pattern = 4 x 4 in / 10 x 10 cm (wet-blocked swatch).
Adjust needle size to obtain correct gauge if necessary.

Pattern repeat of basic motif = 8 sts and 8 rows.

Please read instructions completely before beginning to knit.

SMALL BLOCKS
Mittens

With Color 2 and dpn, CO 56 sts. Divide sts onto dpn and join. Work garter stitch in the round: Beginning and ending with purl rnds, alternate purl and knit rnds until 5 purl rnds show on the RS.

Attach Color 1 and knit 2 rnds.

Knit right and left mittens, following chart.

Right mitten: Begin thumb gusset 1 st before beginning of rnd (green line on chart).

Left mitten: Begin thumb gusset 1 st after last st of rnd (red line on chart).

THUMB GUSSET Only one thumb gusset is knitted on each mitten.

Right mitten: Work thumb gusset sts framed in green (do not knit gusset sts on opposite side of chart).

Left mitten: Work thumb gusset sts framed in red (do not knit gusset sts on opposite side of chart).

Tip: Pm at each side of thumb gusset and work gusset sts between markers following chart.

On Row 37 of chart, place gusset's 12 sts + 8 sts from mitten hand onto 2 safety pins or stitch holder (see green line for right mitten and red line for left mitten). CO 8 new sts with backward loops over the gap. Continue following chart.

Work Rows 38–45 4 times (for a longer or shorter mitten, work more or fewer rnds).

NOTE: There is one more dec at side so pattern willbe even at top of hand.

Tip: If you add a half repeat in length, reverse both halves of the top of the mitten so the pattern stays consistent.

After completing all charted rows for mitten, cut yarn and draw end through rem 6 sts.

THUMB Pick up the 8 sts cast on over thumbhole, slide the 20 sts

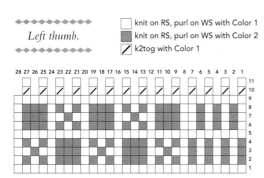

from holder to dpn, and divide these 28 sts onto 3 dpn.

The round for the thumb begins at the first of the 8 sts picked up over thumbhole.

Work thumb for right mitten following chart for right thumb, and for left mitten following chart for left thumb.

Left thumb.

	knit on RS, purl on WS with Color 1
	knit on RS, purl on WS with Color 2
/	k2tog with Color 1

Right thumb.

Work Rows 1–8 2 times.

You can make the thumb longer or shorter as desired.

Continue following the chart through the top shaping.

After completing final rnd, cut yarn and draw end through rem 14 sts.

Make the second mitten the same way, placing thumb correctly.

Weave in all ends neatly on WS. Wash mittens in lukewarm water with wool-safe soap. Rinse if necessary. Roll in towel and then lay flat to dry.

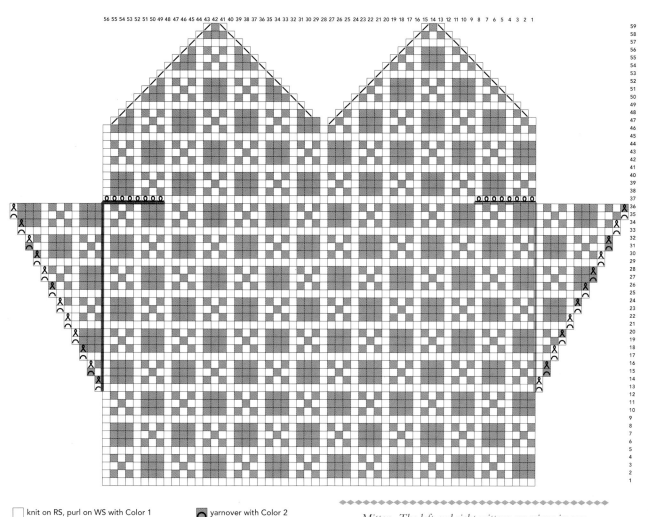

	knit on RS, purl on WS with Color 1
	knit on RS, purl on WS with Color 2
	ssk with Color 1
	k2tog with Color 1
	yarnover with Color 1
	yarnover with Color 2
	k1tbl into yo with Color 1
	k1tbl into yo with Color 2
	backward loop CO with Color 1

Mitten. The left and right mittens are mirror images. The left mitten's thumb gusset is marked in red, and the right mitten's thumb gusset in green.

SMALL BLOCKS
Socks

With Color 2 and dpn, CO 64 sts. Divide sts onto 4 dpn and join. Work garter stitch in the round: Beginning and ending with purl rnd, alternate purl and knit rnds until 5 purl rnds show on RS.

Attach Color 1 and knit 2 rnds.

Knit right and left socks, following the chart. The chart shows half of sock; knit other half the same way.

Work Rows 1–8 5 times.

Between Rows 8 and 9 of chart, work heel over sts 1-32 with scrap yarn (red line on chart; do not work sts 33-64). Slide sts back to left needle and knit in pattern.

Work foot around all sts, following the chart, and repeat Rows 9–16 6 times (if you want a longer or shorter sock, work repeat more or fewer times).

Work Rows 17–34 of chart and then begin toe shaping.

There is one additional decrease on the left side of the chart, so that the pattern will work out evenly for the sock toe.

After completing toe, cut yarn and draw end through rem sts.

HEEL Pick up 32 sts below scrap yarn at heel and 32 sts above. Carefully remove scrap yarn.

With Color 1, knit the 32 sts from leg. Now start rnd with the sts that begin the sole. Work heel as for

toe, beginning at Row 18 of chart.

Make sure that pattern motifs match, although there will be a half stitch shift along the sts that were facing the sole below the scrap yarn.

After completing heel, cut yarn and draw end through rem sts.

Make second sock the same way.

Weave in all ends neatly on WS. Wash the socks in lukewarm water with wool-safe soap. Rinse if necessary. Roll in towel and then lay flat to dry.

- □ knit on RS, purl on WS with Color 1
- ■ knit on RS, purl on WS with Color 2
- ⟍ ssk with Color 1
- ⟋ k2tog with Color 1

Half of heel. Knit other half the same way. Heel placement is shown in red.

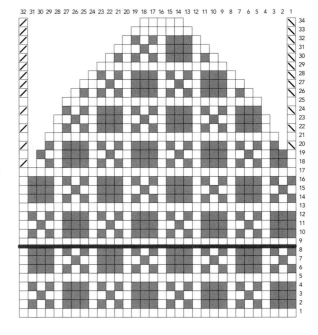

Sock.

SMALL BLOCKS
Hat

With Color 2 and short circular, CO 140 sts. Join, being careful not to twist cast-on row. Pm for beginning of rnd. Work garter stitch in the round: Beginning and ending with purl rnd, alternate purl and knit rnds until 5 purl rnds show on RS.

Attach Color 1 and work in pattern, following chart. The chart only shows a fourth of hat; knit the other three sections the same way.

After Row 1 inc, there will be 160 sts around.

Work Rows 8–15 of chart 4 times.

Beginning at Row 16, decrease as shown on chart. When sts no longer fit around circular, change to dpn.

Cut yarn and draw end through 24 rem sts.

Weave in all ends neatly on WS. Wash hat in lukewarm water with wool-safe soap. Rinse if necessary. Roll in towel and then place over an inflated balloon (size equivalent to head of wearer) to dry.

TASSEL With Color 1 and dpn, knit an I-cord with 4 sts and 60 rows. Make tassel with Color 2 and sew securely to end of I-cord. Sew other end of I-cord securely to tip of hat. For more details, see "Tassels, pompoms, and I-cords" on page 13.

A fourth of the hat. Knit the other three sections the same way. Work Rows 8–15 (in red) 4 times.

	knit on RS, purl on WS with Color 1		⟍	ssk with Color 1		⟰	k3tog with Color 1
	knit on RS, purl on WS with Color 2		⟋	k2tog with Color 1		Ⓞ	backward loop CO with Color 1

SMALL BLOCKS
Original pattern

This small block motif can be found in several Nordic countries and in other regions around the Baltic Sea. It has been recorded in many books and described as typically Norwegian, Danish, Swedish, Estonian, and Finnish. It's easy to conclude that this is an old motif, and has traveled a long way over time.

These mittens came from Estonia and were bought by the Nordic Museum in Stockholm in 1901.

SUN WHEEL

Mittens and hat

The sun wheel is a very old motif that is thought of as a traditional pattern from Gotland, though we can't be certain it originated on the island. It's equally effective as a dark motif against a light background.

FINISHED MEASUREMENTS
Mittens: total length 10¾ in / 27 cm; thumbhole to tip 5½ in / 14 cm; hand circumference 8 in / 20.5 cm.
Hat: circumference 21½ in / 54 cm; length 11¾ in / 30 cm.

YARN
CYCA #2 (sport/baby) Östergötland Visjögarn (328 yd/300 m / 100 g).
Substitute yarns: Rauma Finullgarn or Gammelserie, Blacker Elegance or Shetland 4-ply, Jamieson's Double Knitting, or any yarn which knits to the same gauge.

YARN AMOUNTS
Mittens: Color 1 (Red), 50 g; Color 2 (White), 50 g.
Hat: Color 1 (Red), 50 g; Color 2 (White), 50 g; for the tassel, Color 1 (Red), 10 g.

NOTIONS
2 large safety pins or stitch holder; smooth contrast-color scrap yarn.

NEEDLES
U.S. size 1-2 / 2.5 mm: set of 5 dpn and 16 in / 40 cm circular.

GAUGE
31 sts and 32 rnds in pattern = 4 x 4 in / 10 x 10 cm (wet-blocked swatch).
Adjust needle size to obtain correct gauge if necessary.

Pattern repeat = 22 sts and 22 rows.

With a pattern repeat as large as this one, it's more difficult to adjust the sizing using more or fewer repeats without splitting motifs. If you need to change the size, try using yarn of a different weight and/or different needles to get a larger/smaller gauge.

Please read instructions completely before beginning to knit.

SUN WHEEL
Mittens

With Color 1 and dpn, CO 60 sts. Divide sts onto 4 dpn and join.

Work garter stitch in the round: Beginning and ending with purl rnds, alternate purl and knit rnds until 5 purl rnds show on RS.

Attach Color 2 and knit 1 rnd, increasing 6 sts around as follows: (k10, CO 1 with backward loop) = 66 sts.

Knit 2 more rnds with Color 2.

Work right mitten following chart for right mitten, and left mitten following chart for left mitten (pages 52-53). Work Rows 1–10 of chart before beginning thumb gusset on Row 11.

THUMB GUSSET Work Rows 1–24 of right thumb gusset, following chart for right thumb, and left thumb gusset following chart for left thumb.

Place thumb gusset between stitches as indicated on appropriate chart.

Tip: Pm on each side of gusset and work gusset sts between markers.

On Row 35 of chart, place the 12 gusset sts + 8 sts from hand onto safety pins or holder as shown on chart for right/left mitten. CO 8 sts with backward loops over the gap and then continue following mitten chart.

After completing charted rows, cut yarn and draw end through rem sts.

THUMB Puk 8 sts in the backward loops over the thumbhole, slide the 20 sts from

holder to dpn, and divide these 28 sts onto 3 dpn.

The rnd begins with the first of the 8 sts picked up and knitted above thumbhole. The pattern repeat does not end evenly at center back of thumb.

Work right and left thumbs following right and left thumb charts respectively.

Make the thumb longer or shorter as desired.

After completing last charted row, cut yarn and draw end through rem sts.

Make the other mitten the same way, placing thumb correctly.

Weave in all ends neatly on WS. Wash mittens in lukewarm water with wool-safe soap. Rinse if necessary. Roll in towel and then lay flat to dry.

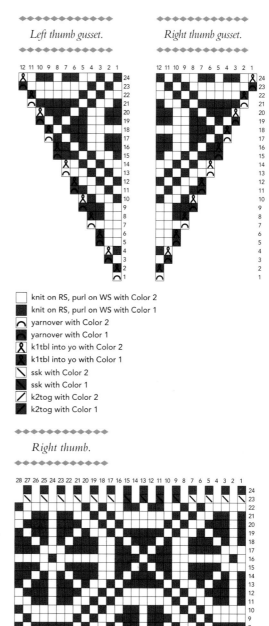

Left thumb gusset.   *Right thumb gusset.*

	knit on RS, purl on WS with Color 2
	knit on RS, purl on WS with Color 1
	yarnover with Color 2
	yarnover with Color 1
	k1tbl into yo with Color 2
	k1tbl into yo with Color 1
	ssk with Color 2
	ssk with Color 1
	k2tog with Color 2
	k2tog with Color 1

Left thumb.   *Right thumb.*

knit on RS, purl on WS with Color 2   knit on RS, purl on WS with Color 1   ssk with Color 1   k2tog with Color 1

backward loop CO with Color 2   backward loop CO with Color 1

66 65 64 63 62 61 60 59 58 57 56 55 54 53 52 51 50 49 48 47 46 45 44 43 42 41 40 39 38 37 36 35 34 33 32 31 30 29 28 27 26 25 24 23 22 21 20 19 18 17 16 15 14 13 12 11 10 9 8 7 6 5 4 3 2 1

| | knit on RS, purl on WS with Color 2 | | knit on RS, purl on WS with Color 1 | | ssk with Color 1 | | k2tog with Color 1 |

| Ω | backward loop CO with Color 2 | | backward loop CO with Color 1 |

SUN WHEEL
Hat

With Color 1 and short circular, CO
160 sts. Join, being careful not to twist
cast-on row. Pm for beginning of rnd.

Work garter stitch in the round:
Beginning and ending with
purl rnds, alternate purl
and knit rnds until 5 purl
rnds show on RS.

Attach Color 2 and work in
St st, increasing 16 sts on the
first rnd as follows: (K10, CO
with 1 backward loop) = 176 sts.

Knit 2 more rnds with Color 2, and
then work in pattern, following chart.

Work Rows 1–22 2 times and then
work Rows 23–70. Change to dpn
when sts no longer fit around circular.

NOTE: The chart only shows half of
hat; knit other half the same way. On
Row 30 of chart, there's an ssk only
on the first half of the hat.

Cut yarn and draw end through rem sts.

TASSEL With Color 1 and dpn, knit
an I-cord with 4 sts and 60 rows.
Make tassel with Color 2 and sew
securely to end of I-cord. Sew other
end of I-cord securely to tip of hat.
For more details, see "Tassels,
pompoms, and I-cords" on page 13.

Weave in all ends neatly on WS.
Wash hat in lukewarm water with
wool-safe soap. Rinse if necessary.
Roll in towel and then place over an
inflated balloon (size equivalent to
head of wearer) to dry.

*Half of hat. Knit the other half the same way, noting that, on
Row 30, there is an ssk only on the first half. Work Rows 1–22
(framed in black) 2 times.*

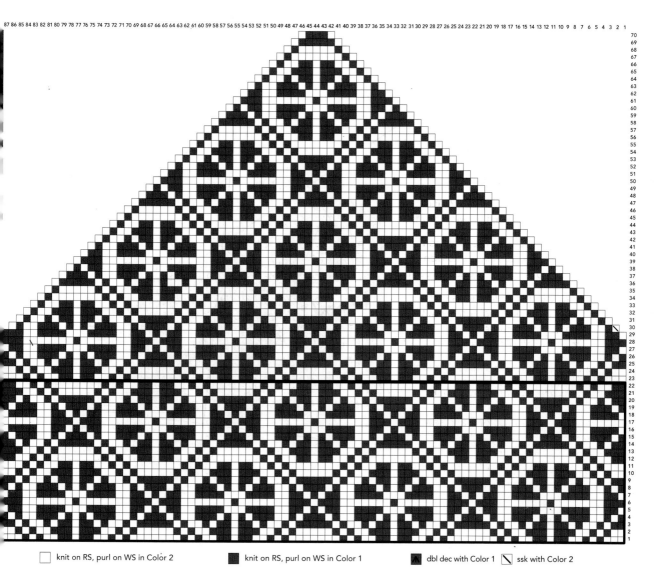

| | knit on RS, purl on WS in Color 2 | | knit on RS, purl on WS in Color 1 | | dbl dec with Color 1 | | ssk with Color 2 |

SUN WHEEL
Original pattern

The sun wheel is considered one of the oldest preserved patterns typical of Gotland. There are several variations, such as this one with the interior cross. Some versions have only the sun wheel.

This pattern is also common in the province of Halland in southwest Sweden, and on the island of land. It can also be found in several other regions. The motif may have traveled to these other areas via garments the Gotland sweater "hags" sold during their visits to Sweden.

The sun wheel is a symbol rooted in antiquity, and there are sources showing that the sun wheel shape was included in rock carvings in Sweden dating to the Bronze Age.

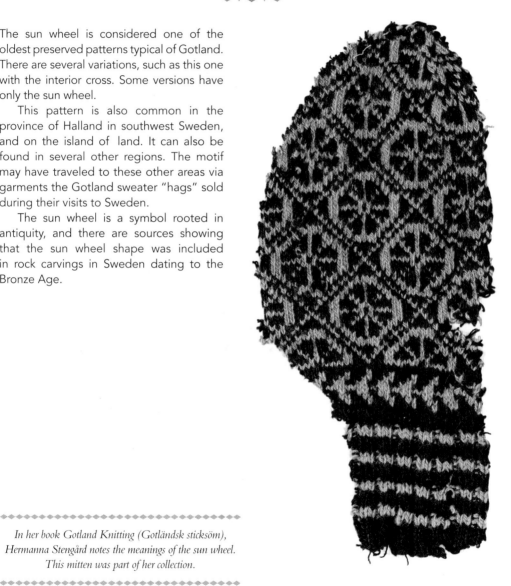

In her book Gotland Knitting (Gotländsk sticksöm), Hermanna Stengård notes the meanings of the sun wheel. This mitten was part of her collection.

LINE DANCE

Mittens, hat, and stockings

This set is a real party! You can change the panels to only men or only women if you like. The small background motif makes the knitting more durable, and the doubled hat brim adds an extra layer of warmth.

FINISHED MEASUREMENTS

Mittens: total length 11½ in / 29 cm; thumbhole to tip 5½ in / 14 cm; hand circumference 7½ in / 19 cm.

Hat: circumference 20½ in / 52 cm; length 9½ in / 24 cm.

Stockings: leg length 15 in / 38 cm; foot length 9 in / 23 cm; foot circumference 7¾ in / 19.5 cm; cuff circumference 11½ in / 29 cm.

YARN

Mittens and hat: CYCA #2 (sport/baby) Östergötland Visjögarn (328 yd/300 m / 100 g; 16 WPI).

Stockings: CYCA #1 (sock) Schachenmayr Regia (230 yd/210 m / 50 g; 20 WPI).

Substitute mitten and hat yarn: Rauma Finullgarn or Gammelserie, Blacker Elegance, or any yarn which knits to the same gauge.

Substitute stocking yarn: Drops Fabel or any yarn which knits to the same gauge.

YARN AMOUNTS

Mittens: Color 1 (White), 60g; Color 2 (Brown), 50g.

Hat: Color 1 (White), 60g; Color 2 (Brown), 50g.

Stockings: Color 1 (White), 120g; Color 2 (Brown), 80g.

NEEDLES

U.S. size 1-2 / 2.5 mm: set of 5 dpn and 16 in / 40 cm circular.

GAUGE

Mittens and hat: 32 sts and 32 rnds in pattern = 4 x 4 in / 10 x 10 cm (wet-blocked swatch).

Stockings: 33 sts and 32 rnds in pattern = 4 x 4 in / 10 x 10 cm (wet-blocked swatch).

Adjust needle size to obtain correct gauge if necessary.

NOTIONS

2 large safety pins or stitch holder; smooth contrast-color scrap yarn.

Pattern repeat, line dance = 16 sts and 14 rows.
Pattern repeat, background = 4 sts and 2 rows.

Please read instructions completely before beginning to knit.

LINE DANCE
Mittens

With Color 1 and dpn, CO 64 sts. Divide sts onto 4 dpn and join. Work 30 rnds in k1, p1 ribbing.

Knit the next rnd, decreasing 4 sts as follows: (ssk, k14) around = 60 sts rem.

Work right mitten following chart for right mitten, and left mitten following chart for left mitten (pages 62-63). Work Rnds 1–2 before beginning thumb gusset on Rnd 3.

THUMB GUSSET Work Rows 1–24 of right thumb gusset following chart for right gusset, and left gusset following chart for left gusset.

Place thumb gusset sts as indicated on chart for each hand respectively.

Tip: Pm on each side of gusset and work gusset sts between markers.

On Row 27 of mitten, place the 12 sts of thumb gusset + 8 sts from hand onto 2 safety pins or a holder, as marked on charts for right/left mitten. CO 8 sts with backward loops over the gap and then continue, following charted pattern.

After completing charted rows (including thumb gusset), cut yarn and draw end through rem 8 sts.

THUMB Work right thumb following chart for right thumb, and left thumb following chart for left thumb. Puk 8 sts with backward loop cast-on over the thumbhole. Slide the 20 thumb sts

Right mitten with single-sided gusset.

- 60 -

+ 8 gusset sts to a needle and then divide these 28 sts onto 3 dpn.

The round for the thumb begins with the first of the 8 sts picked up and knitted above thumbhole.

To align pattern motifs, decrease 1 st on one side of thumbhole and increase 1 st on other side of thumbhole, as indicated on the chart. Repeat Rows 2–3 of chart 9 times.

The thumb can be lengthened or shortened as desired.

After completing last rnd, cut yarn and draw through rem 14 sts.

Make the other mitten the same way, placing thumb correctly.

Weave in all ends neatly on WS. Wash the mittens in lukewarm water with wool-safe soap. Rinse if necessary. Roll in towel and then lay flat to dry.

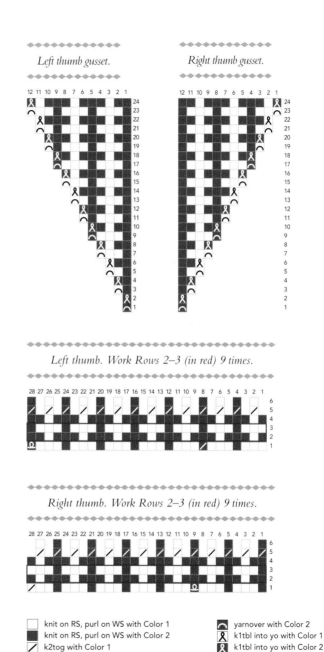

Left thumb gusset.

Right thumb gusset.

Left thumb. Work Rows 2–3 (in red) 9 times.

Right thumb. Work Rows 2–3 (in red) 9 times.

☐ knit on RS, purl on WS with Color 1	⌒ yarnover with Color 2
■ knit on RS, purl on WS with Color 2	☒ k1tbl into yo with Color 1
⁄ k2tog with Color 1	☒ k1tbl into yo with Color 2
⁄ k2tog with Color 2	Ω backward loop CO with Color 2
⌒ yarnover with Color 1	

Left mitten.

knit on RS, purl on WS with Color 1 ▪ knit on RS, purl on WS with Color 2 ◣ ssk with Color 1 ◣ ssk with Color 2

◢ k2tog with Color 1 ◢ k2tog with Color 2 ⋀ dbl dec with Color 1 ⋀ dbl dec with Color 2

Ω backward loop CO with Color 1 Ω backward loop CO with Color 2

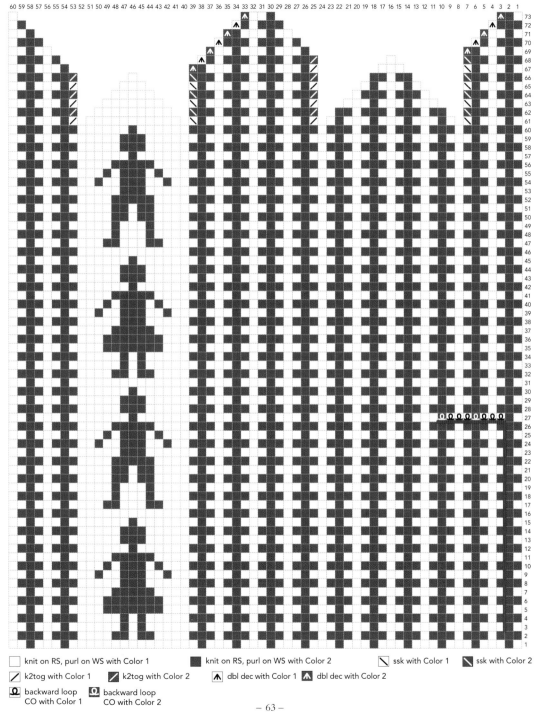

Right mitten.

knit on RS, purl on WS with Color 1	knit on RS, purl on WS with Color 2	ssk with Color 1	ssk with Color 2

k2tog with Color 1	k2tog with Color 2	dbl dec with Color 1	dbl dec with Color 2

backward loop CO with Color 1	backward loop CO with Color 2

LINE DANCE
Hat

16 15 14 13 12 11 10 9 8 7 6 5 4 3 2 1

22
21
20
19
18
17
16
15
14
13
12
11
10
9
8
7
6
5
4
3
2
1

☐ knit on RS, purl on WS with Color 1
■ knit on RS, purl on WS with Color 2

Hat brim. Work repeat a total of 10 times around.

With Color 1 and short circular, CO 140 sts. Join, being careful not to twist cast-on row. Pm for beginning of rnd. Work in k1, p1 ribbing for 4 rnds.

On next rnd, inc: (K7, 1 backward loop CO) around = 160 sts.

Work following chart for hat brim. The chart shows the dancers upside down because the brim will be turned over.

After completing brim chart rows, turn brim inside out and k 3 rnds with Color 1.

Work 6 in / 15 cm in background pattern, following chart for hat crown = repeat Rows 1–2 23 times.

NOTE: The chart shows only a fourth of the hat. Work the other three sections the same way.

Turn the work inside out.

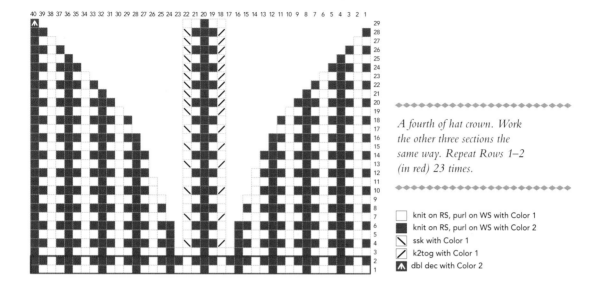

40 39 38 37 36 35 34 33 32 31 30 29 28 27 26 25 24 23 22 21 20 19 18 17 16 15 14 13 12 11 10 9 8 7 6 5 4 3 2 1

29 28 27 26 25 24 23 22 21 20 19 18 17 16 15 14 13 12 11 10 9 8 7 6 5 4 3 2 1

A fourth of hat crown. Work the other three sections the same way. Repeat Rows 1–2 (in red) 23 times.

☐ knit on RS, purl on WS with Color 1
■ knit on RS, purl on WS with Color 2
╲ ssk with Color 1
╱ k2tog with Color 1
⬆ dbl dec with Color 2

Continue crown, following Rows 3–29 of chart. When sts no longer fit around circular, change to dpn.

Tip: *Pm at each of the 8 dec lines, using a different color/style of marker for beginning of rnd.*

Cut yarn and draw end through rem sts.

Turn brim up to the RS and, with MC, puk 1 st in each purl loop from the first purl rnd at the foldline = 160 sts around.

Dec rnd: (K2tog, p1, k1, p1, k1, p1, k1, p1) around, ending with k2tog, p1, k1, p1, k1, p1 = 142 sts rem.

Work 3 more rnds in k1, p1 ribbing. BO loosely in ribbing.

Weave in all ends neatly on WS. Wash the hat in lukewarm water with wool-safe soap. Rinse if necessary. Roll in towel and then place over an inflated balloon (size equivalent to head of wearer) to dry.

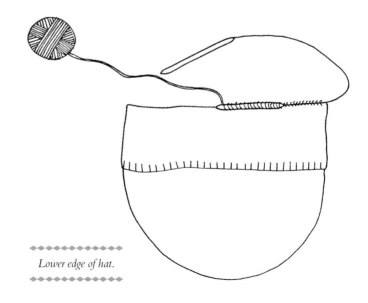

Lower edge of hat.

LINE DANCE
Stockings

With Color 1 and dpn, CO 96 sts. Divide sts over 4 dpn and join.

Work 4 rnds in k1, p1 ribbing.

Knit 2 rnds in St st.

Work cuff, following chart. The rnd begins at center back of stocking.

After completing cuff chart rows, knit 2 rnds in St st.

Tip: To make a wider leg, CO 112 sts and increase the number of repeats in cuff.

Continue stocking cuff as for brim of hat, turning knitting inside out.

On cuff of stockings, dancers are worked right side up so they will be standing correctly when cuff is turned out.

Work background pattern, following "Stocking Leg" chart = repeat Rows 1–2 17 times.

Now begin shaping leg: On every 5th rnd at center back, dec, following Rows 1–20 of chart 4 times (dec 2 sts by working ssk and k2tog respectively on each side of center back stitch 16 times).

Tip: If you began with 112 sts for cuff, begin decreasing after 38 rnds of background pattern and work decreases on every 3rd rnd 24 times.

There should now be 64 sts around. Work Rows 1–2 one more time.

HEEL The heel flap is worked back and forth over the 32 sts on Ndls 1

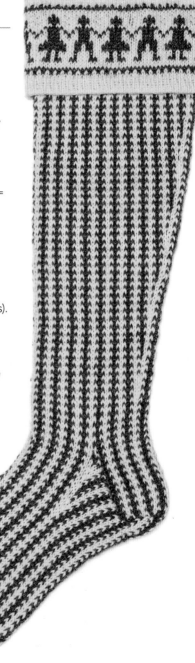

Stocking cuff. The pattern panel on the leg. Repeat a total of 6 times around.

16 15 14 13 12 11 10 9 8 7 6 5 4 3 2 1

22 21 20 19 18 17 16 15 14 13 12 11 10 9 8 7 6 5 4 3 2 1

☐ knit on RS, purl on WS with Color 1
■ knit on RS, purl on WS with Color 2

and 4. Do not work the instep sts, which are on Ndls 2 and 3.

The center back of the stocking is also the center of the heel flap. To align the pattern, cut the yarn after completing the last rnd before flap. The row now begins with the sts on Ndl 4. Move all sts from Ndls 4 and 1 onto the same dpn and then work the heel flap, following the chart. Repeat Rows 3–4 11 times.

After working 24 rows for the heel flap, shape the heel turn, following Rows 5–14 of chart.

The heel should now have 23 sts. Move the first 12 sts to Ndl 4 and leave the rem 11 sts on Ndl 1.

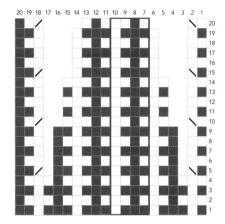

| | knit on RS, purl on WS with Color 1 |
| | knit on RS, purl on WS with Color 2 |
| ssk with Color 1 |
| k2tog with Color 1 |

Stocking leg. Dec at center back. Repeat pattern framed in red as many times as you can around. Work Rows 1–20 4 times.

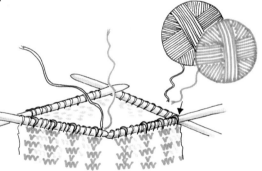

Heel flap. Cut yarn and begin flap rows on Ndl 4.

Heel flap. Repeat Rows 3–4 (in red) 11 times.

	knit on RS, purl on WS with Color 1
	knit on RS, purl on WS with Color 2
	p2tog with Color 1
	p2tog with Color 2
	k2tog with Color 1
	k2tog with Color 2
	slip 1 in Color 1
	slip 1 in Color 2
	k1 and turn to WS
	p1 and turn to RS
	backward loop CO with Color 2

Heel gusset.

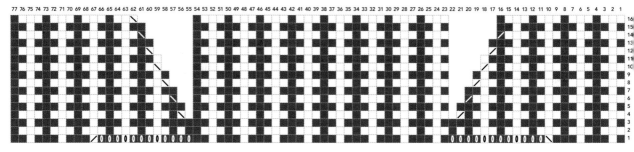

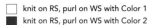
knit on RS, purl on WS with Color 1
knit on RS, purl on WS with Color 2

ssk with Color 1
ssk with Color 2

k2tog with Color 1
k2tog with Color 2

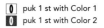
puk 1 st with Color 1
puk 1 st with Color 2

HEEL GUSSET Cut yarn and begin the round on Ndl 1.

Work in the round, including the instep sts on Ndls 2 and 3.

Work following gusset chart above. The decreases are placed at end of Ndl 1 and beginning of Ndl 4.

FOOT Work following foot chart below, working Rows 1–2 16 times or until foot is desired length before toe. Work toe shaping following Rows 3–18 of chart.

Cut yarn and draw end through rem sts.

Fold stocking cuff to RS and puk 1 st in each purl loop from 1st purl round at foldline = 96 sts around.

Work in k1, p1 ribbing for 4 rnds. BO loosely in ribbing.

Make second stocking the same way.

Weave in all ends neatly on WS. Wash stockings in lukewarm water with wool-safe soap. Rinse if necessary. Roll in towel and then lay flat to dry.

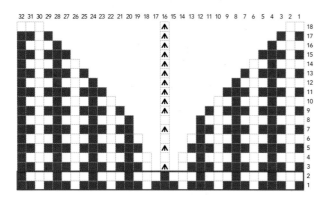

Half of foot. Work other half the same way. Repeat Rows 1–2 (in red) 16 times.

knit on RS, purl on WS with Color 1
knit on RS, purl on WS with Color 2
dbl dec with Color 1

LINE DANCE
Original pattern

Dancing has always been a form of enjoyment all around the world, so it's easy to understand why it has shown up as a motif in knitted patterns.

A line of dancers is featured on these black and white mittens from Selbu in Norway. The design has also been knitted on the Faroe Islands, but its origins are unknown.

You can also use the line dance motif around the edge of a sweater—or why not along the length of a scarf?

These Selbu mittens are now in the Folk Museum in Oslo, Norway. Maybe these mitten remnants were saved just for the patterns?

DAMASK

Gloves, collar, and hat

A beautiful, lustrous mohair yarn was chosen for this set for its whiteness. These accessories have a crocheted edging, which can be omitted if you prefer a more "knitted" look. The single-color relief stitch pattern is worked with knit and purl stitches.

FINISHED MEASUREMENTS

Gloves: total length 11 in / 28 cm; thumbhole to tip 4¾ in / 12 cm; hand circumference 7 in / 18 cm.
Collar: width at neck 15 in / 38 cm; length 6¾ in / 17 cm; lower circumference 32¼ in / 82 cm.
Hat: circumference at lower edge: 21¼ in / 54 cm; length 8¼ in / 21 cm.

YARN

CYCA #1 (fingering/baby) Ateljé Norrgården Gårdens 2-ply mohair yarn (393 yd/360 m / 100 g; 18 WPI).
Substitute yarns: Rauma Finullgarn or Blacker British Wool & Mohair, or any yarn which knits to the same gauge.

YARN AMOUNTS

Gloves: 70 g.
Collar: 60 g.
Hat: 60 g.

NOTIONS

10 safety pins or stitch holders; 6 mother-of-pearl buttons, approx. ¼ in / 8 mm in diameter, for collar.

NEEDLES AND CROCHET HOOK

U.S. size 0 / 2 mm: set of 5 dpn and 16 in / 40 cm circular. U.S. size A / 2 mm: crochet hook.

GAUGE

34 sts and 44 rnds in St st = 4 x 4 in / 10 x 10 cm (wet-blocked swatch).
Adjust needle size to obtain correct gauge if necessary.

Pattern repeat = 6 sts and 21 rows.

Please read instructions completely before beginning to knit.

DAMASK
Gloves

With dpn, CO 72 sts and divide sts evenly over 4 dpn; join.

Work in pattern, following chart. The pattern repeat is in red.

After completing charted rows, k 5 rnds in St st (10 rnds for a longer glove).

On the next rnd, dec 4 sts evenly spaced around: (k2tog, k16) 4 times = 68 sts rem.

Knit 10 rnds.

On the next rnd, decrease 4 sts evenly spaced around: (k8, k2tog, k7) 4 times = 64 sts rem.

THUMB GUSSET Place thumb gusset for right glove between 2nd and 5th sts on Ndl 1 and, for left glove, between 60th and 63rd sts on Ndl 4.

Tips: Pm at each side of gusset sts and work gusset within the markers. If you want a longer thumb gusset, increase on every 4th rnd, which will make the gusset 11 rows longer.

When there are 24 thumb gusset sts between the markers, place these sts on 2 long safety pins or stitch holder. CO 2 sts with backward loops above gap.

Damask pattern. The repeat is marked with red.

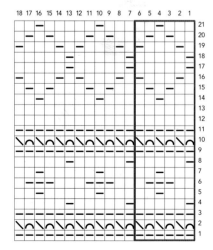

Thumb gusset.

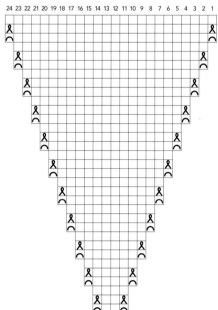

- ☐ knit on RS, purl on WS
- — purl on RS, knit on WS
- ⌢ yarnover
- ╲ ssk
- Ⴟ k1tbl in yo

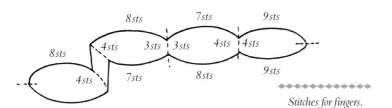

8 sts

8 sts   4 sts   3 sts   3 sts   7 sts   9 sts

4 sts   4 sts

8 sts

4 sts   7 sts   8 sts   9 sts

8 sts

Stitches for fingers.

Work 18 rnds in St st (or 21 rnds if you want a longer glove).

Now divide for fingers.

FINGERS Double-check that thumb is placed correctly in relation to fingers before you knit fingers. Place sts for right thumb on Ndl 1 and sts for left thumb on Ndl 4. That way you can work the fingers for either glove following the same instructions below. Divide sts for fingers onto 3 dpn.

Stitches for little finger: K24. Place 8 + 8 sts onto safety pins. CO 4 new sts at base of ring finger and then complete the rnd.

Knit 3 rnds.

Stitches for ring finger: Place the 4 new sts + 8 + 7 sts on safety pins.

Stitches for middle finger: Place 7 + 8 sts on safety pins.

Knit index finger: K9, CO 4 sts, k9. Knit the 22 sts of index finger for 30 rnds or to desired length.

Next rnd: K2tog around.

Knit 1 rnd.

Cut yarn and draw end through rem sts.

Knit middle finger: Place held middle finger sts onto dpn. CO 3 sts between middle and ring fingers; puk 4 sts at base of index finger = 22 sts. Knit 34 rnds or to desired length.

Shape tip and finish as for index.

Knit ring finger: Place held ring finger sts onto dpn. Puk 3 sts between middle and ring fingers = 22 sts. Knit 30 rnds or to desired length.

Shape tip and finish as for index.

Knit little finger: Place held little finger sts onto dpn. Puk 4 sts at base of ring finger = 20 sts. Knit 26 rnds or to desired length.

Shape tip and finish as for index.

THUMB Puk 2 sts in cast-on sts at thumbhole; move the 24 held sts from safety pins to dpn and divide these 26 sts onto 3 dpn.

The rnd begins with the 2 sts that were picked up above thumbhole.

Knit 22 rnds or to desired length.

Shape tip and finish as for index.

CROCHETED EDGING Crochet an edging around lower edge of glove cuffs, working through back

loops as follows: *(1 sc, 1 dc) in same st, (1 dc, 1 sc) in next st, 1 sl st into next st; rep from * around.

Make the other glove the same way, placing thumb correctly.

Weave in all ends neatly on WS. Wash gloves in lukewarm water with wool-safe soap. Rinse if necessary. Roll in towel and then lay flat to dry.

Edging. Crochet in back loops.

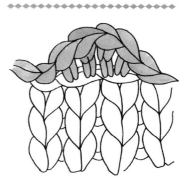

DAMASK
Collar

With short circular, CO 121 sts. Do not join.

Work back and forth, following "Collar, top panel" chart. Row 1 is on WS.

The pattern repeat is framed in red.

Continue working back and forth in St st.

Rows 22–23: St st.

Row 24: Increase 20 sts spaced as follows: K3, (1 backward loop CO, k6), end with 1 backward loop, k4 = 141 sts total.

Rows 25–33: St st.

Row 34: Increase 20 sts spaced as follows: K4, (1 backward loop CO, k7), end with 1 backward loop, k4 = 161 sts total.

Rows 35–43: St st.

Row 44: Increase 20 sts spaced as follows: K4, (1 backward loop CO, k8), end with 1 backward loop, k5 = 181 sts total.

Rows 45–53: St st, in the round: join and CO 1 st at center front. This st should be purled on RS throughout. The rnd begins after this purl st (pm) = 182 sts total.

Row 54: Increase 24 sts around: K7, (1 backward loop CO, k7), end k7 = 206 sts total.

Rows 55–60: Knit around; end with p1.

Work around, following "Collar, lower panel" chart; BO loosely.

You might think it isn't worth it to bind off when you'll work the crocheted edging next. However, if you don't bind off, the edge will be too loose. Do not cut yarn.

CROCHETED EDGING Crochet edging around lower edge of collar, working through back loops of bound-off sts as follows: *(1 sc, 1 dc) in same st, (1 dc, 1 sc) in next st, 1 sl st into next st; rep from * around.

Crochet button loops on the side where buttonholes would be (on right side for women's clothing). Begin at base of placket and work up to collar top. Work 26 sc along edge.

Work crocheted edging (as above) all around neckline, but work only 1 st in each collar st so collar won't be too wide. Finish rnd with 26 sc down left side of placket.

On right side, make button loops as follows: (3 sc, ch 3, skip 1 st) 6 times and end with 2 sc.

Weave in all ends neatly on WS. Sew on buttons opposite loops.

Wash collar in lukewarm water with wool-safe soap. Rinse if necessary. Roll in towel and then lay flat to dry.

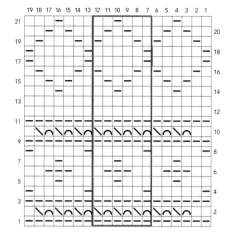

Collar, top panel.
Follow chart; work
the repeat (in red)
18 times.

	knit on RS, purl on WS
—	purl on RS, knit on WS
⌐	yarnover
＼	ssk

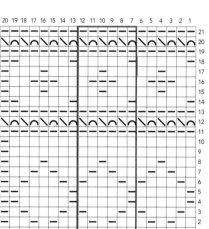

Collar, lower panel.
Follow chart; work
the repeat (in red)
32 times.

	knit on RS, purl on WS
—	purl on RS, knit on WS
⌐	yarnover
＼	ssk

Crochet button loops,
starting at A and
ending at B.

DAMASK
Hat

With short circular, CO 150 sts. Join, being careful not to twist cast-on row; pm for beg of rnd.

Tip: For a larger hat, CO 162 sts; for a smaller hat, CO 138 sts.

Work in the round, following "Damask Pattern" chart as for beginning of gloves on page 72. The pattern repeat is in red.

After completing charted rows, continue in St st until hat measures 6 in / 15 cm.

CROWN SHAPING Pm after every 25th st (for smaller size, pm after every 23rd st; for larger size, pm after every 27th st). The crown has 6 sections.

Dec rnd: (Slm, k1, ssk, k until 2 sts before next marker, k2tog) around.

Dec this way every 3rd rnd (= 2 rnds St st, 1 dec rnd) until 90 sts rem.

Change to dpn and dec as prev *on every other rnd* until 18 sts rem.

Cut yarn and draw end through rem sts.

CROCHETED EDGING Crochet edging around lower edge of hat, working through back loops of cast-on sts as follows: *(1 sc, 1 dc) in same st, (1 dc, 1 sc) in next st, 1 sl st into next st; rep from * around.

Weave in all ends neatly on WS. Wash hat in lukewarm water with wool-safe soap. Rinse if necessary. Roll in towel and then place over an inflated balloon (size equivalent to head of wearer) to dry.

DAMASK
Original pattern

In the mid-1800s, it was common for people to wear white cotton gloves to church. At that time, cotton was a luxury fiber. It was much whiter than wool and very desirable for Sunday outfits.

The newly knitted garments were inspired by relief-stitch sweaters made in Skåne and Denmark. In Denmark, this type of knit was called "damask" and brought to mind woven damask fabric with single-color patterns. In Skåne, sweaters with this patterning were called "spede" sweaters; the Danish versions were called "night sweaters."

Unlike woven damask fabric, knitted damask designs can even be worked as diagonal patterns.

Gloves for Sunday wear were often knitted with white cotton yarn. These gloves, made with mohair, are whiter than wool, but they are not as lustrously white as cotton gloves.

WATER RUNNER

Mittens, hat, and socks

In Estonia, this motif is called "the water runner" and resembles an insect (a water strider). The original mittens have their roots in Finland and are red and white, but they would be pretty in many other color combinations. The fine wavy edging forms cuffs for the mittens, socks, and hat.

FINISHED MEASUREMENTS

The instructions include two sizes: women's (men's). Measurements and instructions for the men's size are within parentheses.
Mittens: total length 11½ (12¾) in / 29 (32) cm; thumbhole to mitten tip 5½ (6½) in / 14 (16.5) cm; hand circumference 8 (8) in / 20 (20) cm.
Hat: circumference 20½ (22) in / 52 (56) cm; length 8¼ in / 24 (24) cm.
Socks: leg length 5½ (6¾) in / 14 (17) cm; foot length 8¾ (10¾) in / 22 (27) cm; foot circumference 8¾ (8¾) in / 22 (22) cm.

YARN

Mittens and hat: CYCA #0 (lace/light fingering) Design Club DK Duo (591 yd/540 m / 100 g; 21 WPI).
Socks: CYCA #1 (sock) Lang Jawoll (459 yd/420 m / 100 g; 21 WPI).
Substitute mitten and hat yarn: Geilsk Tynd uld (Fine Wool), Isager Tvinni, or any yarn which knits to the same gauge.
Substitute sock yarn: Schachenmayr Regia, Drops Fabel, or any yarn which knits to the same gauge.

YARN AMOUNTS

Mittens: Color 1 (Red), 50 g; Color 2 (White), 50 g.
Hat: Color 1 (Red), 50 g; Color 2 (White), 50 g.
Socks: Color 1 (Red), 50 g; Color 2 (White), 50 g.

NOTIONS

Smooth contrast-color scrap yarn.

NEEDLES

U.S. size 0 / 2 mm: set of 5 dpn, 16 in / 40 cm circular.

GAUGE

Mittens and hat: 42 sts and 38 rnds in 2-color pattern = 4 x 4 in / 10 x 10 cm (wet-blocked swatch).
Socks: 38 sts and 38 rows in 2-color pattern = 4 x 4 in / 10 x 10 cm (wet-blocked swatch).
Adjust needle size to obtain correct gauge if necessary.

Pattern repeat = 14 sts and 22 rows for the 2-color pattern; 18 sts and 24 rows for the chevron border.

Please read instructions completely before beginning to knit.

WATER RUNNER
Mittens

With Color 2 and dpn, CO 108 (108) sts. Divide sts onto 4 dpn and join.

Knit 1 rnd and then work the chevron cuff.

CHEVRON CUFF Work around in St st, following "Chevron Cuff" chart below and working in color sequence as follows:

With Color 2, work Rnds 1–2 6 times.

With Color 1, work Rnds 1–2 2 times.

With Color 2, work Rnds 1–2 2 times.

With Color 2, work Rnds 3–6 once.

To arrange sts for water runner pattern, move first st on each ndl to previous ndl so it will be last on previous ndl. There should now be 84 sts around.

Next, work following chart for mitten, beginning on Row 12 (Row 1). The women's size begins on Row 12 so pattern will have a complete repeat at top of mitten. The men's size has 11 extra rows so it will end at the same point.

The chart shows half of mitten. Work other half the same way, except for thumb placement. The ssk in Color 1 on Row 84 is made only once.

RIGHT THUMBHOLE On Row 45 (34) of chart, k first 21 sts (green line on chart) with scrap yarn. Slide sts back to left ndl and knit in pattern.

LEFT THUMBHOLE On Row 45 (34) of chart, k last 21 sts of Ndl 2 (blue line on chart) with scrap yarn. Slide sts back to left ndl and knit in pattern.

Continue following the chart, shaping top as shown. Don't forget that the ssk on Row 84 is worked at only one side (both sizes).

When 12 sts rem, cut yarn and draw end through rem sts.

THUMB Pick up 21 sts below scrap yarn and 21 sts above. Carefully remove scrap yarn.

Divide these 42 sts onto 3 dpn.

Work following chart for thumb and beginning at Row 12 (Row 1) of chart. The pattern won't match up on back of thumb.

When 10 sts rem, cut yarn and draw end through rem sts.

Chevron cuff. At the start, the repeat is 18 sts across and is repeated 6 times around the mitten.

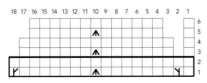

18 17 16 15 14 13 12 11 10 9 8 7 6 5 4 3 2 1

☐ knit on RS, purl on WS
⋀ dbl dec
⅄ inc 1 st with LLI
Γ inc 1 st with RLI

– 80 –

Thumb. The repeat for right thumb is in green; for left thumb, in blue. Each thumb has 3 repeats around.

Key:
- knit on RS, purl on WS with Color 2
- knit on RS, purl on WS with Color 1
- dbl dec with Color 1
- ssk with Color 1

Make second mitten the same way, placing thumb correctly.

Weave in all ends neatly on WS. Wash mittens in lukewarm water with wool-safe soap. Rinse if necessary. Roll in towel and then lay flat to dry.

Half of mitten. Placement of right thumb is marked in green; left thumb, in blue. Begin on Row 12 (1), depending on size desired.

WATER RUNNER
Hat

With Color 2 and short circular, CO 252 (288) sts. Join, being careful not to twist cast-on row. Pm for beginning of rnd. Knit 1 rnd and then work chevron brim.

CHEVRON BRIM Work around in St st, following "Chevron Brim" chart on next page and working in color sequence as follows:

With Color 2, work Rnds 1–2 6 times.

With Color 1, work Rnds 1–2 2 times.

With Color 2, work Rnds 1–2 2 times.

With Color 2, work Rnds 3–6 once.

To arrange sts for water runner pattern, k1 and pm for new start of rnd. There should now be 196 (224) sts around.

Work following chart for hat, working Rows 1–22 2 times (both sizes).

Shape crown, following Rows 23–54 of chart (both sizes). There are 7 (8) decrease sections.

When sts no longer fit around circular, change to dpn.

When 14 (16) sts rem, cut yarn and draw end through rem sts.

One section of hat. Work the other 6 (7) sections the
same way. The repeat is framed in black.

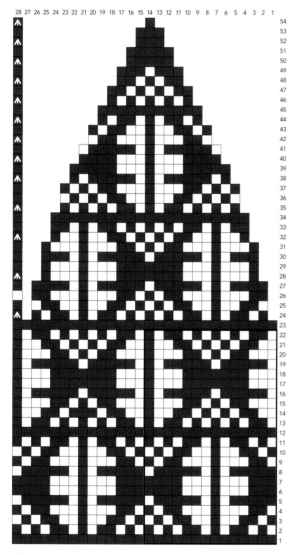

*If you think the hat's too small,
wash it and let it dry on an
inflated balloon (size equivalent
to head of wearer).*

□ knit on RS, purl on WS with Color 2
■ knit on RS, purl on WS with Color 1
⋀ dbl dec with Color 1

Chevron brim. At the start, the repeat
is 18 sts across and is worked 14 (16)
times around the hat.

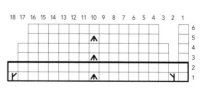

□ knit on RS, purl on WS
⋀ dbl dec
Ƴ inc 1 st with LLI
Ƴ inc 1 st with RLI

WATER RUNNER
Socks

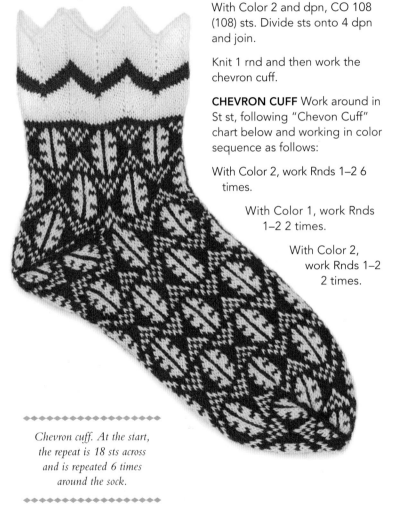

Chevron cuff. At the start, the repeat is 18 sts across and is repeated 6 times around the sock.

With Color 2 and dpn, CO 108 (108) sts. Divide sts onto 4 dpn and join.

Knit 1 rnd and then work the chevron cuff.

CHEVRON CUFF Work around in St st, following "Chevon Cuff" chart below and working in color sequence as follows:

With Color 2, work Rnds 1–2 6 times.

With Color 1, work Rnds 1–2 2 times.

With Color 2, work Rnds 1–2 2 times.

With Color 2, work Rnds 3–6 once.

Knit 1 rnd with Color 1.

To arrange sts for water runner pattern, move first st on each ndl to previous ndl so it will be last on previous ndl. There should now be 84 sts around.

Work following Rows 1–27 (Rows 12–22 + 1–27) on sock chart. The sizes begin at different points so there will be a complete pattern repeat at toe for each size.

Knit right and left socks, following chart. The chart shows half of sock; knit other half the same way except for the ssk with Color 1, which is worked only once as toe shaping begins on Row 51.

On Row 28, work heel over sts 1–42 with scrap yarn (black line on chart). Slide sts back to left ndl and k in pattern. Both socks are worked alike.

Work foot, following Rows 28–49 2 times (Rows 28–49 3 times), and then begin toe shaping. Don't forget: the ssk on Row 51 is worked on only one side (both sizes).

18 17 16 15 14 13 12 11 10 9 8 7 6 5 4 3 2 1

	knit on RS, purl on WS
⋀	dbl dec
Y	inc 1 st with LLI
Γ	inc 1 st with RLI

— 84 —

When 16 sts rem, cut yarn and draw end through rem sts.

HEEL Pick up 42 sts below scrap yarn at heel and 42 sts above. Carefully remove scrap yarn.

Divide these 84 sts onto 4 dpn.

Work heel as for toe, beginning at Row 50 of chart.

When 16 sts rem, cut yarn and draw end through rem sts; tighten.

Make second sock the same way.

Weave in all ends neatly on WS. Wash socks in lukewarm water with wool-safe soap. Rinse if necessary. Roll in towel and then lay flat to dry.

Half of sock. Work other half the same way.

	knit on RS, purl on WS with Color 2
	knit on RS, purl on WS with Color 1
⋀	dbl dec with Color 1
◣	ssk with Color 1

WATER RUNNER
Original pattern

The Finnish photographer and journalist IK Inha made many journeys around Finland at the turn from the nineteenth to the twentieth century to document Finnish country life. In 1894, he visited the Russian village of Akonlahti, near the Finnish border, and he found these mittens, which awakened his interest. He bought the mittens from their owner and she told him she had made them for her grandmother, whose father had come from Finland. The grandmother's Finnish background informed these pretty pattern-knitted mittens—and perhaps some homesickness did, too. They were most likely knitted around 1860.

*These mittens are now part of the Finnish-Ugric collection
in the National Museum of Finland.*

SELBU PATTERN

Gloves and hat

This glove and hat set is based on Selbu mitten patterns.
The star's rays on the gloves continue out into the fingers
so the vines follow the rays. The crown of the hat sports
all the small motifs from the gloves and the pretty star
makes a striking border.

FINISHED MEASUREMENTS

Gloves: total length 9¾ in / 25 cm; thumbhole to
tip 5 in / 12.5 cm; hand circumference 8 in / 20 cm.
Hat: circumference 20½ in / 52 cm; length 9¾ in
/ 25 cm.

YARN

CYCA #2 (sport/baby) Östergötland Visjögarn
(328 yd/300 m / 100 g; 16 WPI).
Substitute yarns: Rauma Finullgarn or
Gammelserie, Blacker Shetland 4-ply, or any
yarn which knits to the same gauge.

YARN AMOUNTS

Gloves: Color 1 (White), 60 g; Color 2 (Black), 40 g.
Hat: Color 1 (White), 60 g; Color 2 (Black), 40 g.

NOTIONS

8 large safety pins or stitch holders; smooth
contrast-color scrap yarn.

NEEDLES

U.S. size 1-2 / 2.5 mm: set of 5 dpn and 16 in / 40
cm circular.

GAUGE

32 sts and 32 rnds in 2-color knitting = 4 x 4 in
/ 10 x 10 cm (wet-blocked swatch).
Adjust needle size to obtain correct gauge if
necessary.

Pattern repeat, star = 31 sts and 31 rows.
Pattern repeat, background pattern = 4 sts
and 6 rows.

Please read instructions completely before
beginning to knit.

SELBU PATTERN
Gloves

With Color 1 and dpn, CO 56 sts and divide evenly over 4 dpn; join.

Work around in k1, p1 ribbing for 6 rnds.

Knit 2 rnds with Color 1.

Work cuff, following charted pattern below.

After completing charted rows, knit 2 rnds with Color 1.

Knit right glove following right glove chart, and left glove following left glove chart.

THUMB GUSSET Work thumb gusset as shown on chart. The gusset begins with 1 st and is framed in Color 2 on each side.

Tip: Pm at outside of gusset sts and work gusset within markers.

On Row 17 of chart, k the 12 sts (red line on both right and left glove charts) with scrap yarn. Slide sts back to left ndl and k in pattern. Continue to end of glove chart.

When cuff and hand charts (including thumb gusset) have been worked, begin the fingers.

Instructions continue on page 94.

Half of glove cuff. Work other half the same way.

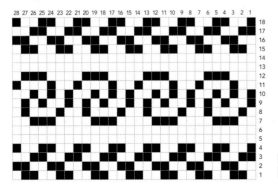

☐ knit on RS, purl on WS with Color 1

■ knit on RS, purl on WS with Color 2

Right glove and gusset with star and background patterns.

☐ knit on RS, purl on WS with Color 1   ■ knit on RS, purl on WS with Color 2   Ω backward loop CO with Color 1

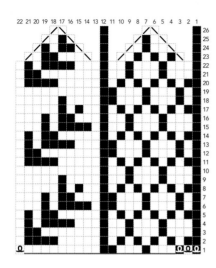

Left index finger.

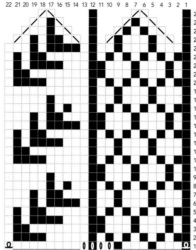

Left middle finger.

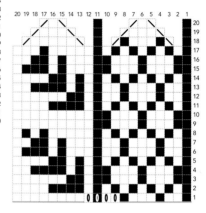

Left little finger.

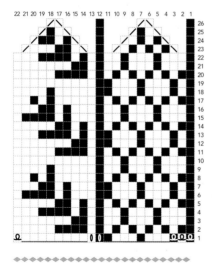

Left ring finger.

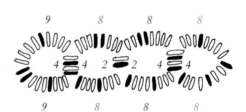

Left glove fingers.
Index finger stitch count
is in red, middle finger in
green, ring finger in lilac,
and little finger in blue.

Left thumb.

	knit on RS, purl on WS with Color 1
■	knit on RS, purl on WS with Color 2
╱	k2tog with Color 1
╲	ssk with Color 1
0	puk 1 st with Color 1
0	puk 1 st with Color 2
Ω	backward loop CO with Color 1
Ω	backward loop CO with Color 2

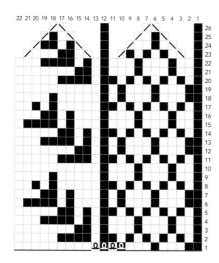

Right index finger.

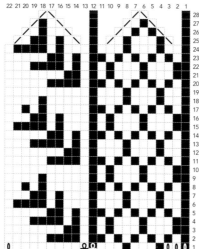

Right middle finger.

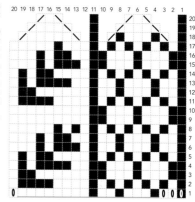

Right little finger.

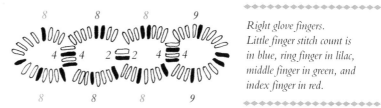

*Right glove fingers.
Little finger stitch count is
in blue, ring finger in lilac,
middle finger in green, and
index finger in red.*

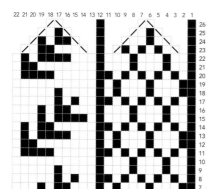

Right ring finger.

Right thumb.

	knit on RS, purl on WS with Color 1
■	knit on RS, purl on WS with Color 2
/	k2tog with Color 1
\	ssk with Color 1
0	puk 1 st with Color 1
0	puk 1 st with Color 2
Ω	backward loop CO with Color 1
Ω	backward loop CO with Color 2

Selbu gloves continued from page 90.

FINGERS Place stitches for each finger, as shown on charts for gloves (page 91), on safety pins.

CO the number of sts between the fingers, following illustrations on pages 92-93.

Begin each finger on palm. The colored lines at bottom of each chart for fingers show how many stitches are held on safety pins and can be checked against colored lines on chart for each glove.

Sometimes you'll need to increase and pick up sts at the beginning of a finger chart. If rnd begins with an inc, make the inc at end of rnd. Increases are only shown at beginning of chart for ease of charting.

Divide sts onto 3 dpn and adjust sts after first rnd so rnd begins at 1st st on chart—that will make charts easier to read.

THUMB Pick up 12 sts below scrap yarn and 12 sts above. Carefully remove scrap yarn. Divide sts onto 3 dpn.

Knit right and left thumbs following corresponding chart.

Make second glove the same way, making sure thumb and fingers are placed correctly.

Weave in all ends neatly on WS. Wash the gloves in lukewarm water with wool-safe soap. Rinse if necessary. Roll in towel and then lay flat to dry.

One section of hat. Knit the other four sections the same way.

	knit on RS, purl on WS with Color 1
■	knit on RS, purl on WS with Color 2

/	k2tog with Color 1
\	ssk with Color 1
⋏	dbl dec with Color 1

SELBU PATTERN
Hat

With Color 1 and circular, CO 160 sts. Join, being careful not to twist cast-on row. Pm for beg of rnd.

Work 6 rnds in k1, p1 ribbing.

Knit 2 rnds with Color 1.

Work following hat chart (page 94).

NOTE: The chart shows one section of hat; work the other four sections the same way.

When sts no longer fit around circular, change to dpn.

Tip: *Pm at start of each section, with a different color/style of marker at beg of rnd.*

After completing charted rows, cut yarn and draw end through rem 10 sts.

Weave in all ends neatly on WS. Wash hat in lukewarm water with wool-safe soap. Rinse if necessary. Roll in towel and then place over inflated balloon (size equivalent to head of wearer) to dry.

SELBU PATTERN
Original pattern

The motifs on these gloves are traditional designs from Selbu in Norway. The classic Selbu patterns can be traced back to the 1850s, but are recognized far from Norway's borders. Selbu mittens often have a small pattern on the palm, a larger star pattern on the back of the hand, and another motif on the thumb.

The gloves are part of Hermanna Stengård's collection of Gotland knitting from the early 1920s. It's possible that the gloves were never intended to be part of the collection, but now we can appreciate the fact that these lovely gloves were saved so we can witness how patterns travel to new places.

Selbu is near Trondheim, Norway, an important harbor city. Maybe this is how these gloves came to be in Hermanna Stengård's Gotland collection—was there a sailor who took them home to Gotland for his beloved? Beautiful designs often travel a long way.

ENGAGEMENT PATTERN

Gloves

These are based on an old pair of gloves knitted for an engaged couple. It was common for a bride to knit gloves for her fiancé, and sometimes also for the wedding party. This pattern looks just as good in wool or in cotton.

FINISHED MEASUREMENTS

The instructions include two sizes: women's (men's). Measurements and instructions for the men's size are within parentheses.
Gloves: total length 9½ (10¾) in / 24 (27) cm; thumbhole to glove tip 4¾ (5½) in / 12 (14) cm; hand circumference 8 (8¾) in / 20 (22) cm.

YARN

CYCA #1 (fingering/baby) CaMaRose Pima cotton (437 yd/400 m / 100 g, 24 WPI).
Substitute yarns: Sandnes Mandarin Petit or any yarn which knits to the same gauge.
If you prefer wool gloves, I recommend Jamieson's Spindrift, Geilsk Tynd uld (fine wool), Rauma Røros Lamb's wool (Lamullgarn), or any yarn which knits to the same gauge.

NOTIONS

10 large safety pins or stitch holders.

YARN AMOUNTS

Color 1 (White), 75 (80) g; Color 2 (Red), 25 (30) g.

NEEDLES

U.S. size 0 / 2 mm: set of 5 dpn.

GAUGE

36 sts and 44 rnds in 2-color pattern = 4 x 4 in / 10 x 10 cm (wet-blocked swatch).
32 sts and 44 rnds in St st = 4 x 4 in / 10 x 10 cm (wet-blocked swatch).
Adjust needle size to obtain correct gauge if necessary.

Pattern repeat = 8 sts and 27 rows.

Please read instructions completely before beginning to knit.

ENGAGEMENT PATTERN
Gloves

Gloves in women's and men's sizes.

With Color 2 and dpn, CO 72 (80) sts and divide sts evenly over 4 dpn; join.

Knit 4 rnds in St st.

Purl 1 rnd (= foldline).

Knit 1 rnd.

Work in pattern, following the chart. The pattern repeat is framed in black. Work repeat 9 (10) times around.

After completing charted rows, knit 1 rnd with Color 2.

Turn knitting inside out and begin working around in other direction.

With Color 2, knit 4 rnds.

Change to Color 1; cut Color 2.

On next rnd, dec 8 sts evenly spaced around: *K7, k2tog* (*k8, k2tog*); work * to * around = 64 (72) sts rem.

Knit 20 (25) rnds.

THUMB GUSSET Place thumb gusset for right glove between 2nd and 5th (2nd and 5th) sts on Ndl 1, and for left glove, between 60th and 63rd (68th and 71st) sts on Ndl 4.

Tip: Pm at edges of gusset sts and work gusset within markers.

When gusset has 22 (26) sts, place sts onto 2 long safety pins or stitch holder. CO 2 sts over gap using backward loop CO.

Work 18 (22) rnds in St st.

Now work fingers.

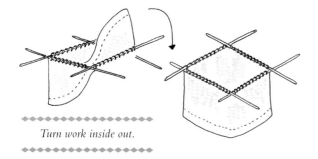

Turn work inside out.

Cuff pattern. The repeat is framed in black and is worked 9 (10) times around.

☐ knit on RS, purl on WS with Color 1
■ knit on RS, purl on WS with Color 2
⌒ yarnover with Color 1
⏿ k1tbl in yo with Color 1

Thumb gusset. Women's size thumb gusset ends at red line. Work all rows for men's size.

FINGERS Double-check that thumb is placed correctly in relation to fingers before you knit fingers. Place sts for right thumb on Ndl 1 and for left thumb on Ndl 4. That way you can work fingers for either glove following the instructions below. Divide sts for fingers onto 3 dpn.

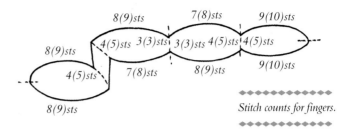

Stitch counts for fingers.

Stitches for little finger: K24 (27). Place 8 + 8 (9+ 9) sts onto safety pins. CO 4 (5) new sts at base of ring finger and then complete rnd.

Knit 3 rnds.

Stitches for ring finger: Place the 4 new sts + 8 + 7 (5 + 9 + 8) sts on safety pins.

Stitches for middle finger: Place 7 + 8 (8 + 9) sts on safety pins.

Knit index finger: K9 (10), CO 4 (5) sts, k9 (10). Knit the 22 (25) sts of index finger for 30 (34) rnds or to desired length.

Next rnd: K2tog around.

Knit 1 rnd.

Cut yarn and draw end through rem sts.

Knit middle finger: Place held middle finger sts onto dpn. CO 3

(3) sts between middle and ring fingers; puk 4 (5) sts at base of index finger = 22 (25) sts total. Knit 34 (38) rnds or to desired length.

Shape tip and finish as for index.

Knit ring finger: Place held ring finger sts onto dpn. Puk 3 (3) sts between middle and ring fingers = 22 (25) sts. Knit 30 (34) rnds or to desired length.

Shape tip and finish as for index.

Knit little finger: Place held little finger sts onto dpn. Puk 4 (5) sts at base of ring finger = 20 (23) sts. Knit 26 (30) rnds or to desired length.

Shape tip and finish as for index.

Knit thumb: Puk 2 sts in cast-on sts at thumbhole; move the 22 (26) held sts from safety pins to dpn

and divide these 24 (28) thumb sts onto 3 dpn.

The rnd begins with the first of the 2 picked-up sts above thumbhole.

Knit 24 (26) rnds or to desired length. K2tog around = 12 (14) sts rem.

Knit 1 rnd.

Cut yarn and draw end through rem sts.

Weave in all ends neatly on WS. Wash gloves in lukewarm water with mild soap. Rinse if necessary. Roll in towel and then lay flat to dry.

ENGAGEMENT PATTERN
Original pattern

The original gloves came from Rackeby in the district of Kålland in Västergötland, Sweden, and were a gift from an engaged woman to her fiancé. These cotton gloves were most likely knitted in the mid-1800s as church gloves. There's clearly much love and anticipation in each stitch from the bride-to-be, along with pride in her ability to present such a fine gift to her fiancé.

This glove, sized to fit a man, belongs to the Nordic Museum in Stockholm, Sweden.

WENDELA AND WENDELA BLUE

Gloves, hat, stockings, and half gloves

What is special about this pattern is that purl stitches are used in the pattern color, becoming a design detail in their own right. It is easy to change the sizing by adding or omitting a single-color row between the small pattern motifs.

FINISHED MEASUREMENTS
Wendela

Gloves: total length 11½ in / 29 cm; thumbhole to tip 5½ in / 13.5 cm; hand circumference 7½ in / 19 cm.

Stockings: leg length 16¼ in / 41 cm, foot length 9 in / 23 cm; foot circumference 8 in / 20 cm; cuff circumference 11¾ in / 30 cm.

Hat: circumference 20½ in / 52 cm; length 9 in / 23 cm.

Wendela Blue

Half gloves: length 8 in / 20 cm; thumbhole to top edge 2½ in / 6 cm; hand circumference 7½ in / 19 cm.

Stockings: leg length 17¼ in / 44 cm, foot length 9 in / 23 cm; foot circumference 8 in / 20 cm; cuff circumference 11¾ in / 30 cm.

YARN

CYCA #1 (sock/fingering/baby) Drops Fabel (224 yd/205 m / 50 g; 21 WPI).

Substitute yarn: Schachenmayr Regia, or any yarn which knits to the same gauge.

YARN AMOUNTS
Wendela

Gloves: Color 1 (White), 50 g; Color 2 (Red) 20 g; Color 3 (Blue), 15 g; Color 4 (Yellow), 10 g.

Stockings: Color 1, 120 g; Color 2, 35 g; Color 3, 25 g; Color 4, 15 g.

Hat: Color 1, 50 g; Color 2, 20 g; Color 3, 15 g; Color 4, 10 g; for pompom, Color 1, 15 g.

Wendela Blue

Half gloves: Color 1 (White), 30 g; Color 2 (Blue), 20 g.

Stockings: Color 1, 120 g; Color 2, 60 g.

NOTIONS

10 large safety pins or stitch holders.

NEEDLES AND CROCHET HOOK

U.S. size 1-2 / 2.5 mm: set of 5 dpn and 16 in / 40 cm circular. U.S. size C-2 / 2.5 mm: crochet hook.

GAUGE

32 sts and 36 rnds in pattern = 4 x 4 in / 10 x 10 cm (wet-blocked swatch).
Adjust needle size to obtain correct gauge if necessary.

Pattern repeat, Wendela = 12 sts, 28 rows.
Pattern repeat, Wendela Blue = 20 sts, 36 rows.
If necessary, end with a partial repeat.

Please read instructions completely before beginning to knit.

WENDELA
Gloves

With Color 1 and dpn, CO 64 sts and divide sts evenly over 4 dpn; join. Work around in k2, p2 ribbing for 30 rnds.

On next rnd, k, decreasing 4 sts evenly spaced around: (Ssk, k14) around = 60 sts rem.

Work right glove following chart for right glove, and left glove following chart for left glove (see pages 108-109).

Work in pattern, following chart. The pattern repeat is in red.

THUMB GUSSET Shape thumb gusset as shown on chart, Rows 6–29.

Work sts of gusset as marked off by black line on each chart (right glove = at beg of Ndl 1; left glove = at end of Ndl 4).

At Row 30 of chart, place the 12 gusset sts + 7 sts from hand onto two long safety pins or stitch holder as shown on chart for right and left gloves respectively. CO 7 new sts using backward loop CO over gap, and continue working

around, following appropriate glove chart.

After completing all charted rows (including gusset), work fingers with Color 1.

FINGERS Double-check that thumb is placed correctly in relation to fingers before knitting fingers.

Place sts for right thumb on Ndl 1 and for left thumb on Ndl 4. That way you can work fingers for either glove following instructions below. Divide sts for the fingers onto 3 dpn.

Stitches for little finger: K22. Place 8 + 8 sts onto safety pins. CO 4 new sts at base of ring finger and then complete rnd.

Knit 3 rnds.

Stitches for ring finger: Place the 4 new sts + 6 + 7 sts on safety pins.

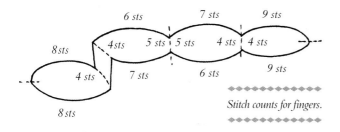

Stitch counts for fingers.

Left glove, including thumb gusset.

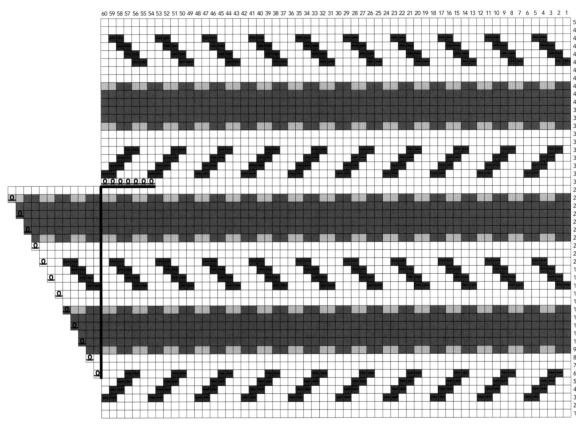

Stitches for middle finger: Place 7 + 6 sts on safety pins.

Knit index finger: K9, CO 4 sts, k9. Knit the 22 sts of index finger for 30 rnds or to desired length.

Next rnd: K2tog around.

Knit 1 rnd.

Cut yarn and draw end through rem sts; tighten and fasten off.

Knit middle finger: Place held middle finger sts onto dpn. CO 5 sts between middle and ring fingers; puk 4 sts at base of index = 22 sts total. Knit 34 rnds or to desired length.

Shape tip and finish as for index.

Knit ring finger: Place the held ring finger sts onto dpn. Puk 5 sts between the middle and ring fingers = 22 sts. Knit 30 rnds or to desired length.

Shape tip and finish as for index.

Knit little finger: Place held little finger sts onto dpn. Puk 4 sts at base of ring finger = 20 sts. Knit 26 rnds or to desired length.

Right glove, including thumb gusset.

	knit on RS, purl on WS with Color 4
	knit on RS, purl on WS with Color 3
	knit on RS, purl on WS with Color 1
	purl on RS, knit on WS with Color 2

Q	backward loop CO with Color 4
Q	backward loop CO with Color 3
Q	backward loop CO with Color 1

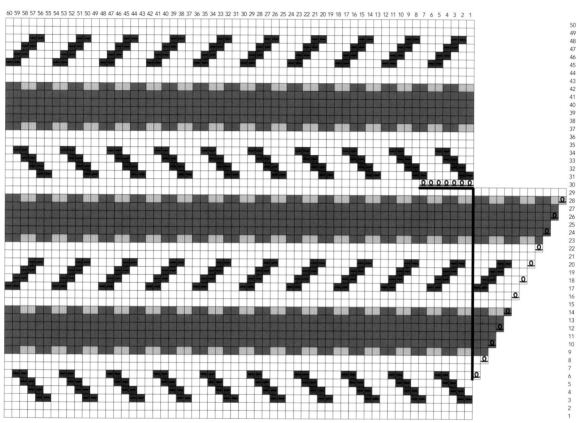

Shape tip and finish as for index.

Knit thumb: Puk 7 sts in cast-on sts above thumbhole; move the 19 held sts from safety pins to dpn and divide the 26 thumb sts onto 3 dpn.

The rnd begins with the first of the 7 sts picked up above thumbhole.

Knit 24 rnds or to desired length.

On next rnd, k2tog around = 13 sts rem.

Knit 1 rnd.

Cut yarn and draw end through rem sts; tighten and fasten off.

Make the other glove the same way,

making sure thumb is placed correctly.

Weave in all ends neatly on WS. Wash gloves in lukewarm water with wool-safe soap. Rinse if necessary. Roll in towel and then lay flat to dry.

WENDELA
Stockings

With Color 1 and dpn, CO 96 sts. Divide sts over 4 dpn and join.

Work 6 rnds k2, p2 ribbing.

Knit 10 rnds in St st.

Work leg following "Stocking leg, top part" chart. The rnd begins with 1st st on chart, which will be at center back of stocking.

Work Rows 1–28 of chart 2 times = 8 repeats around leg.

Now work Rows 1–90 of "Stocking leg, lower part" chart. *At the same time*, shape leg by decreasing at center back on every 5th rnd: K1 (center back st), ssk, k until 2 sts rem, k2tog. After charted rows are completed, 64 sts rem.

Tips: *If dec line at center back leg looks a bit uneven, crochet a row of slip stitches with Color 1 to hide the unevenness. Because the decreases are evenly spaced, pattern will not match at center back. The crocheted line makes this somewhat less obvious. Make sure that the slip sts do not pull in the stocking leg, and that the sts are not too big.*

◆◆◆◆◆◆◆◆◆◆◆◆◆

Crochet slip stitch.

◆◆◆◆◆◆◆◆◆◆◆◆◆

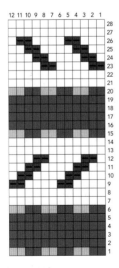

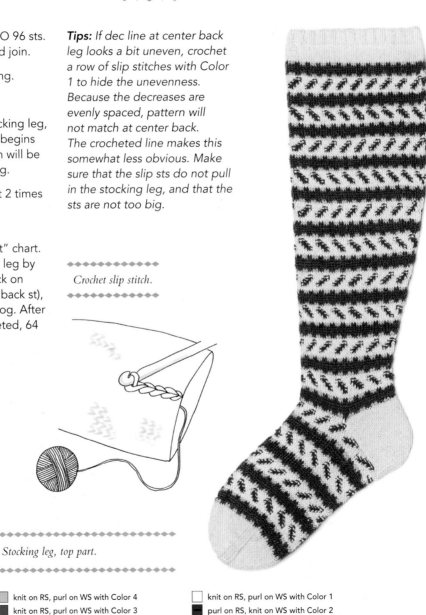

◆◆◆◆◆◆◆◆◆◆◆◆◆◆◆◆◆◆◆◆◆◆◆

Stocking leg, top part.

◆◆◆◆◆◆◆◆◆◆◆◆◆◆◆◆◆◆◆◆◆◆◆

☐ knit on RS, purl on WS with Color 4

■ knit on RS, purl on WS with Color 3

☐ knit on RS, purl on WS with Color 1

■ purl on RS, knit on WS with Color 2

Stocking leg, lower part. Work repeat (framed in black) twice.

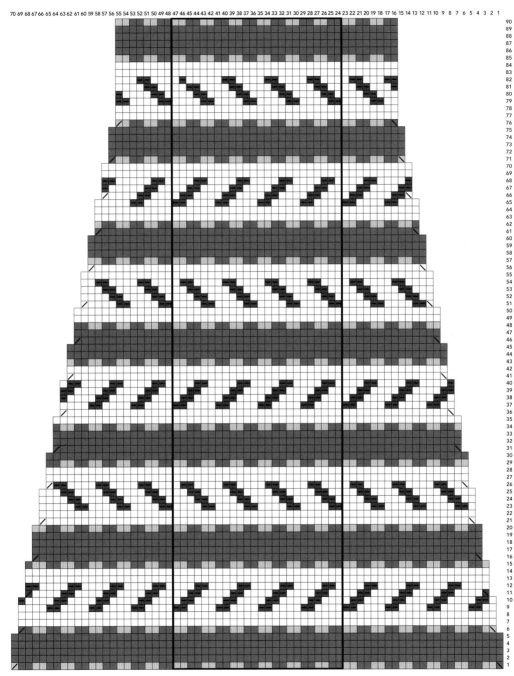

70 69 68 67 66 65 64 63 62 61 60 59 58 57 56 55 54 53 52 51 50 49 48 47 46 45 44 43 42 41 40 39 38 37 36 35 34 33 32 31 30 29 28 27 26 25 24 23 22 21 20 19 18 17 16 15 14 13 12 11 10 9 8 7 6 5 4 3 2 1

90 89 88 87 86 85 84 83 82 81 80 79 78 77 76 75 74 73 72 71 70 69 68 67 66 65 64 63 62 61 60 59 58 57 56 55 54 53 52 51 50 49 48 47 46 45 44 43 42 41 40 39 38 37 36 35 34 33 32 31 30 29 28 27 26 25 24 23 22 21 20 19 18 17 16 15 14 13 12 11 10 9 8 7 6 5 4 3 2 1

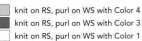 knit on RS, purl on WS with Color 4

knit on RS, purl on WS with Color 3

knit on RS, purl on WS with Color 1

 purl on RS, knit on WS with Color 2

k2tog with Color 4

k2tog with Color 3

 k2tog with Color 2

k2tog with Color 1

ssk with Color 4

 ssk with Color 3

ssk with Color 2

ssk with Color 1

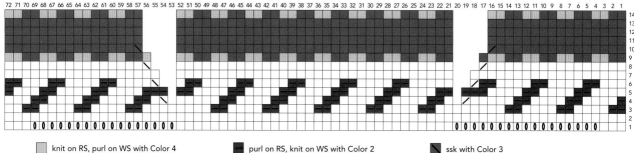

▨ knit on RS, purl on WS with Color 4	■ purl on RS, knit on WS with Color 2	◪ ssk with Color 3
■ knit on RS, purl on WS with Color 3	╱ k2tog with Color 3	◩ ssk with Color 1
□ knit on RS, purl on WS with Color 1	╱ k2tog with Color 1	0 puk 1 st with Color 1

Foot. Work repeat
(framed in black) 5
times.

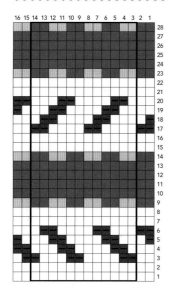

▨ knit on RS, purl on WS with Color 4	
■ knit on RS, purl on WS with Color 3	
□ knit on RS, purl on WS with Color 1	
■ purl on RS, knit on WS with Color 2	

Half of toe. Rnd begins at center of sole.

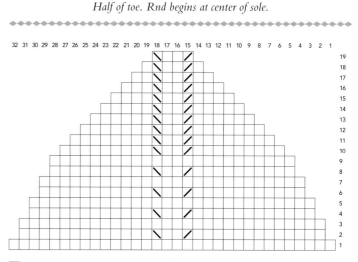

□ knit on RS, purl on WS with Color 1	
╱ k2tog with Color 1	
◣ ssk with Color 1	

*You can adjust sizing by adding
or omitting single-color rounds
between pattern panels.*

HEEL The heel flap is worked back and forth with Color 1 over the 32 sts on Ndls 1 and 4. Do not work the instep sts (Ndls 2 and 3).

The center back of stocking is also center of heel flap. K16 on Ndl 1; turn and p32 (Ndls 1 and 4). Move all sts from Ndls 4 and 1 onto same dpn. The heel flap begins on RS:

Rows 1–16: Work in St st.

Row 17: K12, k2tog, k4, ssk, k12.

Rows 18, 20, 22, and 24: Purl.

Row 19: K11, k2tog, k4, ssk, k11.

Row 21: K10, k2tog, k4, ssk, k10.

Row 23: K9, k2tog, k4, ssk, k9.

Row 25: K14, ssk, turn.

Row 26: Sl 1 purlwise wyf, p4, p2tog, turn.

Row 27: Sl 1 purlwise wyb, k4, k2tog, turn.

Repeat Rows 26–27 until 6 sts rem. Divide rem sts onto Ndls 4 and 1. Work the 3 sts on Ndl 4.

HEEL GUSSET The chart begins with the 1st st at center back. Resume knitting in the round, including the instep sts on Ndls 2 and 3. Puk 17 sts on each side of heel flap. There should now be 20 sts each on Ndls 1 and 4.

Decrease following chart for heel gusset:

At end of Ndl 1, k2tog, and at

beginning of Ndl 4, ssk. Dec the same way on every other row 4 times = 16 sts rem on each dpn or 64 sts total rem.

FOOT Work Rows 1–28 of foot chart (page 112) twice. The pattern will not come out evenly around, but the partial motifs will be on the bottom of the foot.

For longer foot, work a few more rnds in pattern or some extra rnds with Color 1 before starting toe shaping. For shorter foot, end patterning when foot is desired length.

Work toe in Color 1, following toe chart (page 112). The chart shows half of toe; work other half the same way.

Make second stocking the same way.

Weave in all ends neatly on WS. Wash stockings in lukewarm water with wool-safe soap. Rinse if necessary. Roll in towel and then lay flat to dry.

WENDELA
Hat

With Color 1 and short circular, CO 168 sts. Join, being careful not to twist cast-on row; pm for beginning of rnd. Work around in k2, p2 ribbing for 6 rnds, and then work 10 rnds in St st.

Now work Rows 1–28 of "Stocking leg, top part" chart (page 110) twice. The chart shows 1 repeat; there will be 14 repeats around.

Shape crown, following chart below. When sts no longer fit around circular, change to dpn.

Tip: Pm at each of the 14 dec lines, with different color/style of marker for beg of rnd.

Cut yarn and draw end through rem 14 sts; tighten and fasten off.

Weave in all ends neatly on WS. Wash hat in lukewarm water with wool-safe soap. Rinse if necessary. Roll in towel and then place over inflated balloon (size equivalent to head of wearer) to dry.

With Color 1, make pompom and sew securely to top of hat. For details, see "Tassels, pompoms, and I-cords" on page 13.

One section of hat crown. Work the other 6 sections the same way.

■ knit on RS, purl on WS with Color 4
■ knit on RS, purl on WS with Color 3
□ knit on RS, purl on WS with Color 1
◢ k2tog with Color 3
◢ k2tog with Color 1
◣ ssk with Color 3
◣ ssk with Color 1
▲ dbl dec with Color 1

WENDELA BLUE
Half gloves

With Color 1 and dpn, CO 60 sts and divide sts evenly over 4 dpn; join. Work around in k2, p2 ribbing for 6 rnds.

Knit 10 rnds.

Work right glove following chart for right glove, and left glove following chart for left glove. There will be 3 pattern repeats around (framed in black).

THUMB GUSSET Shape thumb gusset as indicated on Rows 12–35 of chart.

Work sts of gusset as marked off by the heavy black line on each chart (right glove = at beg of Ndl 1; left glove = at end of Ndl 4).

On Row 36 of chart, place the 12 gusset sts + 8 sts from hand onto two long safety pins or stitch holder as shown on chart for right and left gloves. CO 8 new sts using backward loop CO over gap and continue working around, following appropriate glove chart.

After completing all charted rows (including thumb gusset), knit 10 rnds with Color 1.

Finish with 6 rnds k2, p2 ribbing. BO in ribbing, making sure bind-off edge is flexible.

Half glove with single-sided gusset.

THUMB Work thumb with Color 1 only. Puk 8 sts in cast-on sts at thumbhole; move 20 held sts from safety pins to dpn and divide these 28 sts onto 3 dpn.

The rnd begins with first of 8 sts picked up above thumbhole.

Knit 10 rnds or to desired length.

Work 6 rnds k2, p2 ribbing. BO in ribbing, making sure bind-off edge is flexible.

Make other half glove the same way, making sure thumb is

positioned correctly.

Weave in all ends neatly on WS. Wash the gloves in lukewarm water with wool-safe soap. Rinse if necessary. Roll in towel and then lay flat to dry.

Left glove. Work repeat (framed in black) 3 times.

Right glove. Work repeat (framed in black) 3 times.

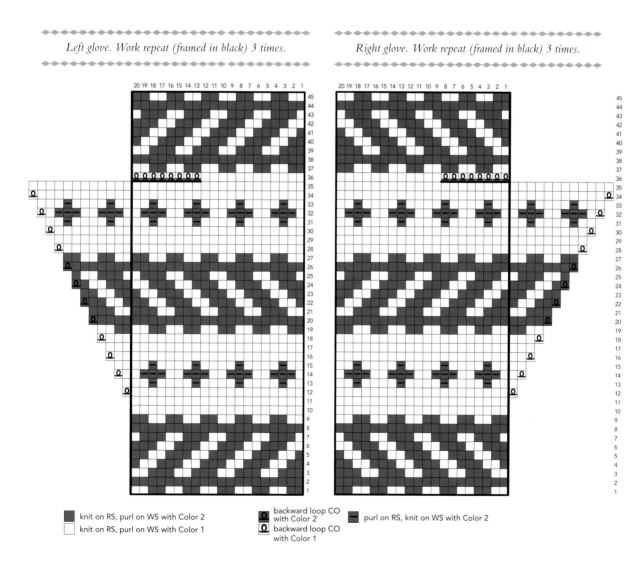

■ knit on RS, purl on WS with Color 2
□ knit on RS, purl on WS with Color 1

☒ backward loop CO with Color 2
☒ backward loop CO with Color 1

━ purl on RS, knit on WS with Color 2

WENDELA BLUE
Stockings

With Color 1 and dpn, CO 96 sts. Divide sts over 4 dpn and join.

Work 6 rnds k2, p2 ribbing.

Knit 10 rnds in St st.

Work leg following "Stocking leg, top part" chart. Rnd begins with 1st st on chart, which will be at center back of stocking.

Work Rows 1–36 of chart, and then work Rows 1–18 once more.

Tip: If dec line at center back leg looks uneven, crochet a row of slip stitches with Color 1 to hide the unevenness. See Wendela stocking (page 110) for details.

Now work Rows 1–99 of "Stocking leg, lower part" chart. *At the same time,* shape leg by decreasing at center back on every 6th rnd: K1 (center back st), ssk, knit until 2 sts rem, k2tog.

After chart is completed, 64 sts rem.

Stocking leg, top part. Work repeat (framed in black) 4 times.

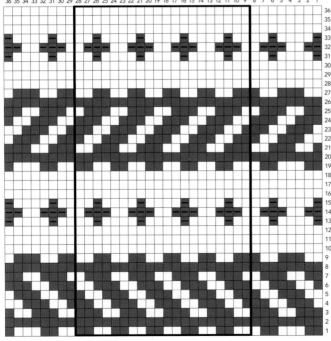

■ knit on RS, purl on WS with Color 2

□ knit on RS, purl on WS with Color 1

▬ purl on RS, knit on WS with Color 2

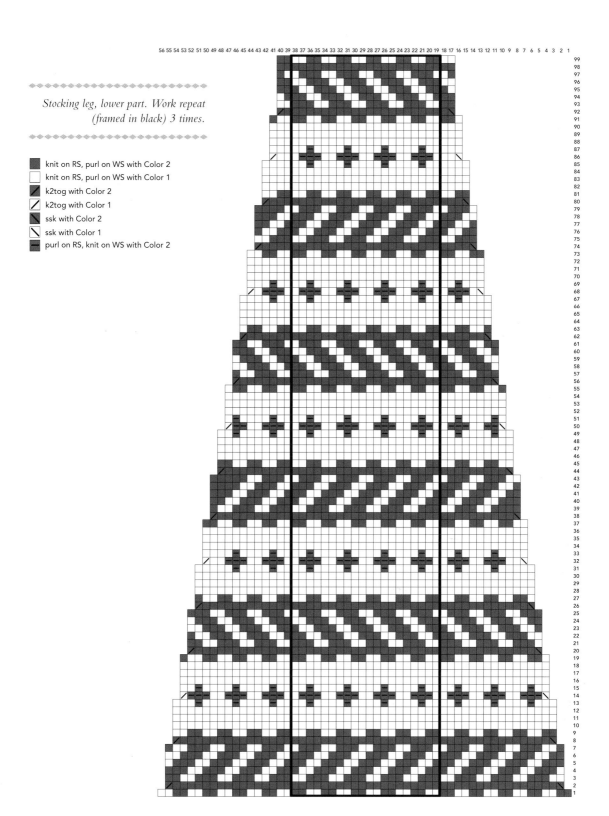

Stocking leg, lower part. Work repeat (framed in black) 3 times.

- ■ knit on RS, purl on WS with Color 2
- □ knit on RS, purl on WS with Color 1
- ◪ k2tog with Color 2
- ◩ k2tog with Color 1
- ◪ ssk with Color 2
- ◱ ssk with Color 1
- ⊟ purl on RS, knit on WS with Color 2

Heel gusset.

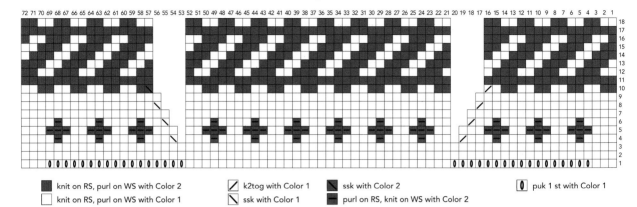

- ■ knit on RS, purl on WS with Color 2
- □ knit on RS, purl on WS with Color 1
- ◤ k2tog with Color 1
- ◣ ssk with Color 1
- ◥ ssk with Color 2
- ▬ purl on RS, knit on WS with Color 2
- 回 puk 1 st with Color 1

HEEL The heel flap is worked back and forth with Color 1 over Ndls 1 and 4, as for the heel flap on Wendela (page 113).

HEEL GUSSET The chart begins with 1st st at center back. Resume knitting in the round, including instep sts on Ndls 2 and 3.

Puk 17 sts on each side of heel flap. There should now be 20 sts each on Ndls 1 and 4.

Decrease following heel gusset chart:

At end of Ndl 1, k2tog, and at beg of Ndl 4, ssk. Dec the same way on every other row 4 times = 16 sts on each dpn or 64 sts total rem.

FOOT Work Rows 1–36 of foot chart and then Rows

1–18 once more. The pattern will not come out evenly around, but partial motifs will be on sole of foot.

For longer foot, work a few more rnds in pattern or some extra rnds with Color 1 before beginning toe shaping. For shorter foot, end patterning when foot is desired length.

Work toe with Color 1 only, following toe chart for Wendela (page 112). The chart only shows half of toe; work other side the same way.

Make second stocking the same way.

Weave in all ends neatly on WS. Wash stockings in lukewarm water with wool-safe soap. Rinse if necessary. Roll in towel and then lay flat to dry.

Foot. Repeat is framed in black.

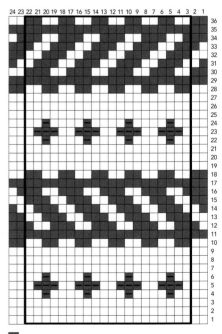

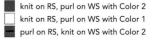

- ■ knit on RS, purl on WS with Color 2
- □ knit on RS, purl on WS with Color 1
- ▬ purl on RS, knit on WS with Color 2

WENDELA AND WENDELA BLUE
Original patterns

In the Norrköping City Museum in Sweden, you'll find these fine stockings knitted by Wendela Olofsson. Wendela and her husband Otto Fredrik moved into Wendela's parents' home, so she lived her entire life in the same house in Brånnestad, in the parish of Å in Östergötland.

Wendela was an expert knitter and it is likely that she did not knit only for her own household.

She knitted the same pattern in various sizes and adjusted the length of the leg and foot by adding single-color rows as necessary. This is clearly seen on the blue stockings, which have the same number of repeats; the stocking with the longer leg has two single-color rounds in each repeat. Some of the stockings also have new heels or toes that were knitted in when the originals wore out.

Wendela's stockings were gifted to the Norrköping City Museum in 1929 by her granddaughter, Aina.

MARGITA

Gloves and hat

This glove and hat set is named after my mother, and was inspired by a pair of gloves she had when she was a child. The turned-up brim makes the hat extra warm. It's easy to adjust the size by changing the thickness of the yarn and the size of the needles.

FINISHED MEASUREMENTS

Gloves: total length 11 in / 28 cm; thumbhole to tip 5¼ in / 13 cm; hand circumference 7 in / 18 cm.

Hat: circumference 20½ in / 52 cm; length 8¾ in / 22 cm.

YARN

CYCA #2 (fingering/baby) Visjögarn from Östergötland (328 yd/300 m / 100 g; 16 WPI).

Substitute yarns: Rauma Finullgarn or Gammelserie, Blacker Shetland 4-ply, or any yarn which knits to the same gauge.

YARN AMOUNTS

Gloves: Color 1 (Red), 50 g; Color 2 (White), 30 g.

Hat: Color 1 (Red), 70 g; Color 2 (White), 30 g; for pompom, Color 1 (Red), 15 g.

NOTIONS

10 large safety pins or stitch holders.

NEEDLES

U.S. size 1-2 / 2.5 mm: 16 in / 40 cm circular and set of 5 dpn.

GAUGE

31 sts and 32 rnds in 2-color knitting = 4 x 4 in / 10 x 10 cm (wet-blocked swatch).
Adjust needle size to obtain correct gauge if necessary.

Pattern repeat, star, gloves = 30 sts and 29 rows.
Pattern repeat, star, hat = 27 sts and 27 rows.
Pattern repeat, glove hands = 18 sts and 4 rows.

Please read instructions completely before beginning to knit.

MARGITA
Gloves

With Color 1 and dpn, CO 56 sts and divide sts evenly over 4 dpn; join.

Work around in k1, p1 ribbing for 30 rnds.

On the next rnd, knit, increasing 1 st at the side = 57 sts.

Knit 6 rnds in St st.

Work right glove following chart for right glove, and left glove following chart for left glove.

THUMB GUSSET Shape thumb gusset as indicated on Rows 1–21 of chart.

Tip: Pm at each side of gusset and work gusset sts between markers.

On Row 22 of chart, place the 8 gusset sts + 8 sts from hand onto two long safety pins or stitch holder as shown on chart for right and left gloves. CO 8 new sts using backward loop CO over gap and continue working

around, following appropriate glove chart.

After completing all charted rows (including thumb gusset), knit 7 rnds with Color 1, decreasing 1 st at side on last rnd = 56 sts rem.

FINGERS Double-check that thumb is placed correctly in relation to fingers.

Place sts for right thumb on Ndl 1 and sts for left thumb on Ndl 4. That way you can work fingers for either glove following the same instructions below. Divide sts for fingers onto 3 dpn:

Stitches for little finger: K21. Place 7 + 7 sts onto safety pins. CO 4 new sts at base of ring finger and then finish rnd.

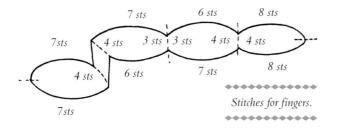

Stitches for fingers.

Left glove and gusset.

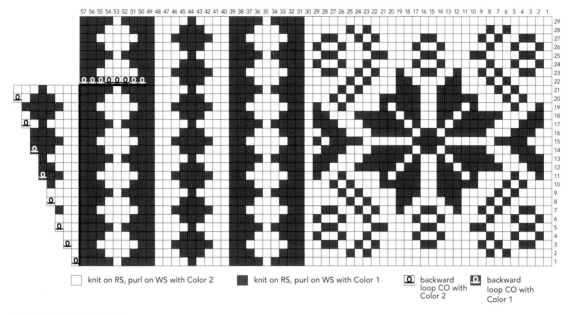

□ knit on RS, purl on WS with Color 2   ■ knit on RS, purl on WS with Color 1   Ω backward loop CO with Color 2   Ω backward loop CO with Color 1

Right glove and gusset.

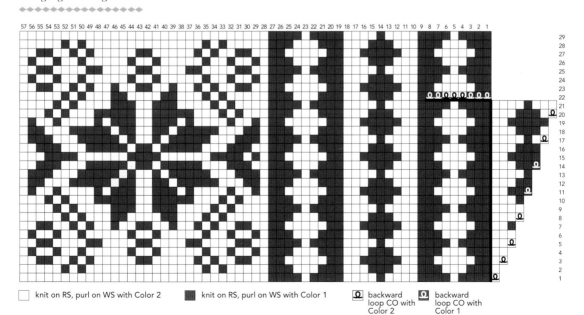

□ knit on RS, purl on WS with Color 2   ■ knit on RS, purl on WS with Color 1   Ω backward loop CO with Color 2   Ω backward loop CO with Color 1

Knit 3 rnds.

Stitches for ring finger: Place the 4 new sts + 7 + 6 sts on safety pins.

Stitches for middle finger: Place 6 + 7 sts on safety pins.

Knit index finger: K8, CO 4 sts, k8. Knit the 20 sts of index finger for 30 rnds or to desired length.

Next rnd: K2tog around.

Knit 1 rnd.

Cut yarn and draw end through rem sts; tighten and fasten off.

Knit middle finger: Place held middle finger sts onto dpn. CO 3 sts between middle and ring fingers; puk 4 sts at base of index finger = 20 sts total. Knit 33 rnds or to desired length.

Shape and finish as for index.

Knit ring finger: Place held ring finger sts onto dpn. Puk 3 sts between middle and ring fingers = 20 sts. Knit 30 rnds or to desired length.

Shape and finish as for index.

Knit little finger: Place held little finger sts onto dpn. Puk 4 sts at base of ring finger = 18 sts. Knit 28 rnds or to desired length.

Shape and finish as for index.

Knit thumb: Puk 8 sts in cast-on sts at thumbhole; move the 16 held sts from safety pins to dpn

and divide these 24 thumb sts onto 3 dpn.

The rnd begins with the first of the 8 sts picked up above thumbhole.

Knit 22 rnds or to desired length.

Shape and finish as for index.

Make other glove the same way, making sure thumb is placed correctly.

Weave in all ends neatly on WS. Wash gloves in lukewarm water with wool-safe soap. Rinse if necessary. Roll in towel and then lay flat to dry.

MARGITA
Hat

With Color 1 and short circular, CO 142 sts. Join, being careful not to twist cast-on row. Pm for beg of rnd. Work in k1, p1 ribbing for 4 rnds.

Next rnd: K2; (k7, 1 backward loop CO) around = 162 sts.

Work following chart for hat brim. The chart shows 1 repeat; work repeat 6 times around.

After completing charted rows, decrease: K2, (k2tog, k6) around = 142 sts rem.

Turn knitting inside out and knit 3 rnds with Color 1.

Tip: Pm at edges of sections for crown, using a different style/color of marker from marker for beginning of rnd.

Decrease another 4 sts on next rnd: K2,

knit on RS, purl on WS with Color 2

knit on RS, purl on WS with Color 1

Turn hat inside out after completing charted pattern and decrease.

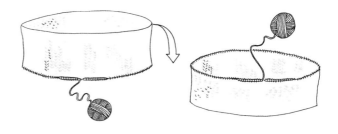

Hat brim. Repeat chart a total of 6 times around.

◆◆◆◆◆◆◆◆◆◆◆◆◆◆◆◆◆◆◆◆◆◆◆◆◆◆◆◆◆◆◆◆◆

*One section of hat crown. Work 5 additional
sections the same way.*

◆◆◆◆◆◆◆◆◆◆◆◆◆◆◆◆◆◆◆◆◆◆◆◆◆◆◆◆◆◆◆◆◆

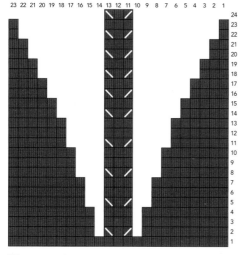

23 22 21 20 19 18 17 16 15 14 13 12 11 10 9 8 7 6 5 4 3 2 1

■	knit on RS, purl on WS in Color 1
⧅	ssk with Color 1
⧄	k2tog with Color 1

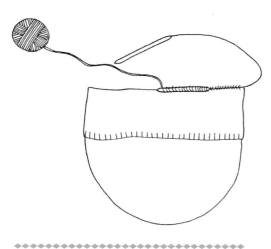

◆◆◆◆◆◆◆◆◆◆◆◆◆◆◆◆◆◆◆◆◆◆◆◆◆◆◆◆◆◆◆◆◆

*Lower edge of hat. Puk 142 sts in
purl loops of foldline.*

◆◆◆◆◆◆◆◆◆◆◆◆◆◆◆◆◆◆◆◆◆◆◆◆◆◆◆◆◆◆◆◆◆

(k33, k2tog) around = 138 sts rem.

Work 6 in / 15 cm with Color 1.

Shape crown following chart. The chart
only shows 1 section; work the other 5
segments the same way.

When sts no longer fit around circular,
change to dpn.

Tip: *Pm at each of the 12 decrease
lines, using a different style/color of
marker from marker for beginning
of rnd.*

Cut yarn and draw end through rem sts.

Turn brim up to RS and, with Color 1,
puk 1 st in each purl loop from first purl
rnd at foldline = 142 sts around.

Work 4 rnds in k1, p1 ribbing. BO
loosely in ribbing.

Weave in all ends neatly on WS. Wash
hat in lukewarm water with wool-safe
soap. Rinse if necessary. Roll in towel
and then place over an inflated balloon
(size equivalent to head of wearer) to
dry.

Make a pompom with Color 1 and sew
securely to top of hat. For details, see
"Tassels, pompoms, and I-cords" on
page 13.

MARGITA
Original pattern

My mother was two years old and lived in Karlskoga in 1941, when my grandmother bought a pair of little gloves for her. I got to see these beloved gloves some years ago and I decided then that I wanted to knit a new pair of adult-size gloves with the same motifs.

The original gloves were machine-knitted and were probably made by one of the many people who had a knitting machine in the kitchen and knitted to sell.

By using a heavier yarn than the originals, I could maintain the proportions of the pattern by adding a few single-color rows.

The small household items in the photo are miniatures that my mother and grandmother both played with when they were little.

STRIPES AND VINES

Mittens and socks

These socks are knitted tightly and are extra strong and firm, just like socks from the "old days." It's easy to change the sizes of the panels by increasing or decreasing the number of single-color rounds between vines. If you are not yet comfortable with two-color stranded knitting, this is a good project to try. The little leaf panel is the only part that has two colors on every row; the rest of the pattern is simply stockinette stripes.

FINISHED MEASUREMENTS

Mittens: total length 10¾ in / 27 cm; thumbhole to mitten tip 5¼ in / 13 cm; hand circumference 7½ in / 19 cm.
Socks: leg length 6 in / 15 cm; foot length 9½ in / 24 cm; foot circumference 8¼ in / 21 cm.

YARN

CYCA #2 (fingering/baby) Rauma Gammelserie (175 yd/160 m / 50 g, 16 WPI).
Substitute yarn: Rauma Finullgarn or any yarn that knits to the same gauge.

YARN AMOUNTS

Mittens: Color 1 (Black), 60 g; Color 2 (Red), 40 g; Color 3 (Blue), 10 g.
Socks: Color 1 (Black), 100 g; Color 2 (Red), 40 g; Color 3 (Blue), 10 g.

NOTIONS

2 large safety pins or stitch holder; smooth contrast-color scrap yarn.

NEEDLES

U.S. size 0 / 2 mm: set of 5 dpn.

GAUGE

32 sts and 38 rnds in pattern = 4 x 4 in / 10 x 10 cm (wet-blocked swatch).
Adjust needle size to obtain correct gauge if necessary.

Pattern repeat = 6 sts and 56 rows.
To adjust length, increase or decrease the number of single-color rounds between bands.

Please read instructions completely before beginning to knit.

STRIPES AND VINES
Mittens

With Color 1 and dpn, CO 60 sts. Divide sts onto dpn and join.

Work 28 rnds in k1, p1 ribbing.

Beginning on next rnd, continue in St st.

Both mittens are worked following the same chart.

Right mitten: Begin thumb gusset with st before 1st st of rnd (marked with green).

Left mitten: Begin thumb gusset with st after last st of rnd (marked with white).

THUMB GUSSET Make only one thumb gusset on each mitten.

Right mitten: Work thumb gusset sts to right of green line on chart. Do not knit sts left of white line.

Left mitten: Work thumb gusset sts to left of white line on chart. Do not knit sts right of green line.

Tip: Pm at edges of gusset and work gusset sts between markers.

On Row 32 of mitten, place 12 sts of thumb gusset + 7 sts from hand onto 2 safety pins or a holder, as marked on chart for mitten. CO 7 sts with backward loop CO over gap and then continue following charted pattern.

After completing charted rows and top shaping, cut yarn and draw end through rem sts.

THUMB With Color 1, puk 7 sts in backward loop CO over thumbhole. Slide the 19 held gusset sts to a needle and then divide these 26 sts onto 3 dpn.

The round for thumb begins at first of picked-up sts above thumbhole.

Knit the 26 thumb sts with Color 1 for 22 rnds or to desired length.

Next rnd: K2tog around.

Knit 1 rnd.

Cut yarn and draw through rem sts.

Make other mitten the same way, placing thumb correctly.

Weave in all ends neatly on WS. Wash mittens in lukewarm water with wool-safe soap. Rinse if necessary. Roll in towel and then lay flat to dry.

Mitten with left and right thumb gussets.

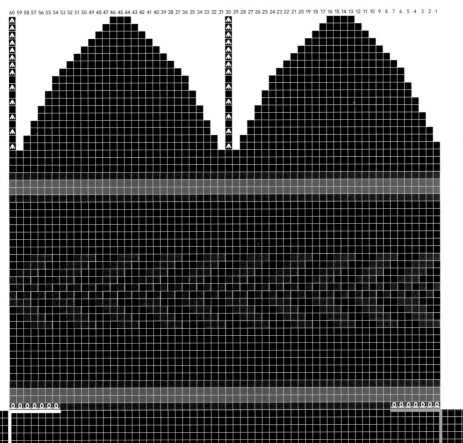

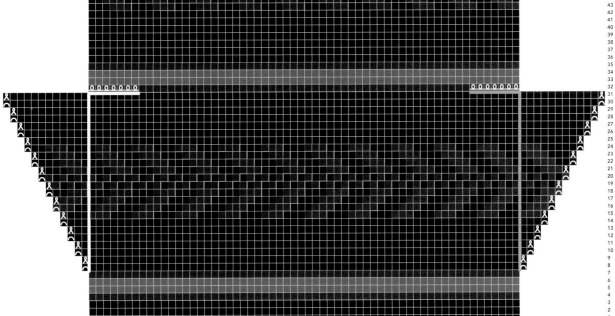

■ knit on RS, purl on WS with Color 2	⋀ dbl dec with Color 1	◣ yarnover with Color 1
■ knit on RS, purl on WS with Color 3	◻ backward loop CO with Color 2	◢ k1tbl with Color 2
■ knit on RS, purl on WS with Color 1	◣ yarnover with Color 2	◢ k1tbl with Color 1

STRIPES AND VINES
Socks

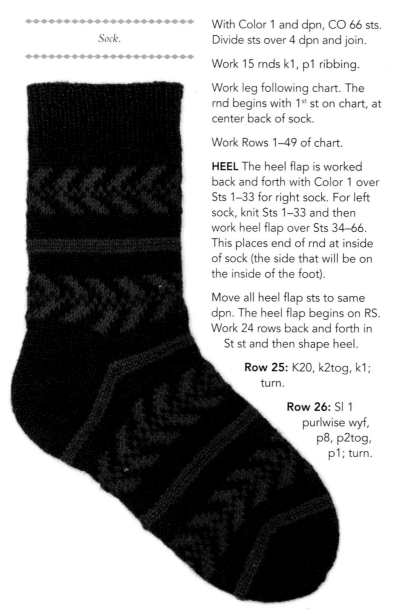

Sock.

With Color 1 and dpn, CO 66 sts. Divide sts over 4 dpn and join.

Work 15 rnds k1, p1 ribbing.

Work leg following chart. The rnd begins with 1st st on chart, at center back of sock.

Work Rows 1–49 of chart.

HEEL The heel flap is worked back and forth with Color 1 over Sts 1–33 for right sock. For left sock, knit Sts 1–33 and then work heel flap over Sts 34–66. This places end of rnd at inside of sock (the side that will be on the inside of the foot).

Move all heel flap sts to same dpn. The heel flap begins on RS. Work 24 rows back and forth in St st and then shape heel.

Row 25: K20, k2tog, k1; turn.

Row 26: Sl 1 purlwise wyf, p8, p2tog, p1; turn.

Row 27: Sl 1 purlwise wyb, k9, k2tog, k1; turn.

Row 28: Sl 1 purlwise wyf, p10, p2tog, p1; turn.

Row 29: Sl 1 purlwise wyb, k11, k2tog, k1; turn.

Row 30: Sl 1 purlwise wyf, p12, p2tog, p1; turn.

Row 31: Sl 1 purlwise wyb, k13, k2tog, k1; turn.

Row 32: Sl 1 purlwise wyf, p14, p2tog, p1; turn.

Row 33: Sl 1 purlwise wyb, k15, k2tog, k1; turn.

Row 34: Sl 1 purlwise wyf, p16, p2tog, p1; turn.

Row 35: Sl 1 purlwise wyb, k17, k2tog, k1; turn.

Row 36: Sl 1 purlwise wyf, p18, p2tog, p1; turn = 21 sts rem on heel flap.

HEEL GUSSET In order for single-color rows before next pattern stripe to match, cut yarn and begin heel gusset at St 34 on chart for right sock, or St 1 on chart for left sock.

Sock. Work Rows 1–49 for leg, and 8–79 for foot.

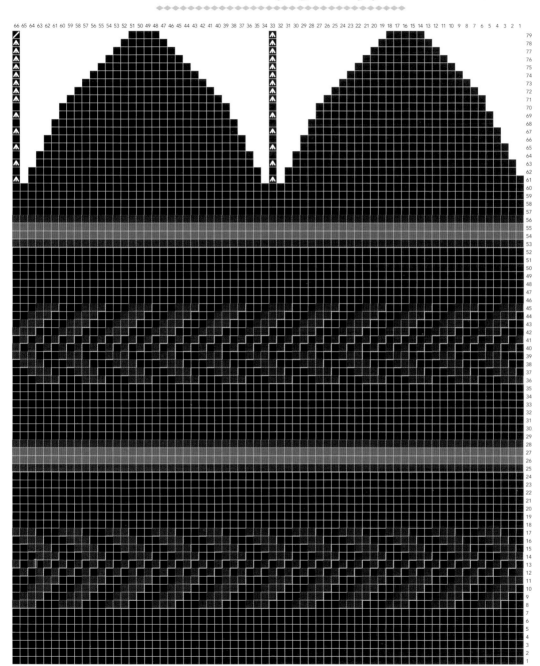

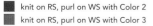 knit on RS, purl on WS with Color 2

knit on RS, purl on WS with Color 3

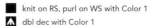 knit on RS, purl on WS with Color 1

dbl dec with Color 1

 k2tog with Color 1

Heel gusset. For right sock, rnd begins at St 34. For left sock, rnd begins at St 1.

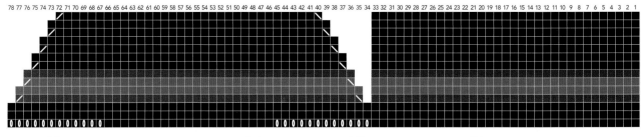

■ knit on RS, purl on WS with Color 2	◥ ssk with Color 2
■ knit on RS, purl on WS with Color 3	◥ ssk with Color 3
■ knit on RS, purl on WS with Color 1	◥ ssk with Color 1

◢ k2tog with Color 2	0 puk 1 st with Color 1
◢ k2tog with Color 3	
◢ k2tog with Color 1	

Resume knitting in the round, including instep sts on Ndls 2 and 3. On first rnd, puk 12 sts on each side of heel flap = a total of 24 sts picked up.

Decrease following heel gusset chart.

FOOT Work following Rows 8–60 of sock chart (page 135). For longer foot, work a few more rnds with Color 1 before beginning toe shaping. For shorter foot, end patterning when foot is desired length.

Work toe with Color 1 only, shaping it following Rows 61–79 of sock chart.

Cut yarn and draw end through rem sts.

Make second sock the same way.

Weave in all ends neatly on WS. Wash socks in lukewarm water with wool-safe soap. Rinse if necessary. Roll in towel and then lay flat to dry.

STRIPES AND VINES
Original pattern

Sometimes only a small piece of a garment is left, but that can be enough to see the beauty in the pattern. At one time, this was part of a pair of warm socks in a pretty, dark brown wool with leafy madder-dyed vines. It was worn by a man from Mattsarfve in Gammelgarn on the Swedish island of Gotland. The striping might have been leftover yarn from another project. Perhaps this remnant was saved because it reminded someone of how the vine pattern was knitted—a textile note.

This sock remnant is in Hermanna Stengård's collection, held by the Gotland County Handicraft Association in Visby.

GRETA'S HAT

Hat

The brim of this hat is worked in entrelac, an exciting
technique where you work a small block at a time. This hat
is an excellent way to use up leftover yarns. The blocks of
entrelac can be knitted with different colors and the rest of the
hat can be made with stripes of leftover yarns all the way up.

FINISHED MEASUREMENTS

Circumference 21 in / 53 cm; length 8¾ in / 22
cm, with brim turned up; brim 2½ in / 6 cm.

YARN

CYCA #0 (lace/light fingering) Geilsk Tynd uld
(314 yd/287 m / 50 g, 21 WPI).
Substitute yarn: Design Club DK Duo, Isager
Tvinni, or any yarn which knits to the same
gauge.

YARN AMOUNTS

Color 1 (Light Green), 90 g; Color 2 (Dark Green),
20 g; for pompom, Color 1 (Light Green), 10 g.

NOTIONS

15 large safety pins or stitch holders.

NEEDLES AND CROCHET HOOK

U.S. size 0 / 2 mm: 16 in / 40 cm circular and
set of 5 dpn. U.S. size A-2 / 2 mm: crochet
hook.

GAUGE

34 sts and 38 rows/rnds in St st = 4 x 4 in /
10 × 10 cm (wet-blocked swatch).
Adjust needle size to obtain correct gauge if
necessary.

The blocks are 10 sts x 20 rows. The brim is 15
blocks around with 12 sts picked up in each
block. The number of stitches for the crown is a
multiple of 10 sts.

Please read instructions completely before
beginning to knit.

GRETA'S HAT
Hat

ENTRELAC

The brim of the hat is knitted using a technique called "entrelac." Each block is worked separately, back and forth.

The structure begins with a row of half blocks leaning right and knitted with Color 1. Next is a tier of blocks in Color 2, leaning left. Stitches are picked up from the long side of the half blocks and knitted together with the stitches on each half block.

To finish, make another tier of half blocks in Color 1, leaning right.

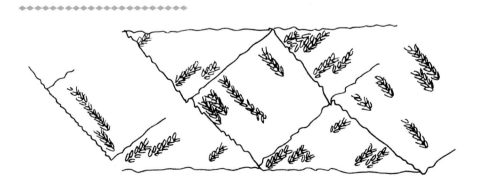

Entrelac.

Half blocks on lower edge of brim.

23 22 21 20 19 18 17 16 15 14 13 12 11 10 9 8 7 6 5 4 3 2 1

44 43
42 41
40 39
38 37
36 35
34 33
32 31
30 29
28 27
26 25
24 23
22 21
20 19
18 17
16 15
14 13
12 11
10 9
8 7
6 5
4 3
2 1

☐ knit on RS, purl on WS
Ω backward loop CO

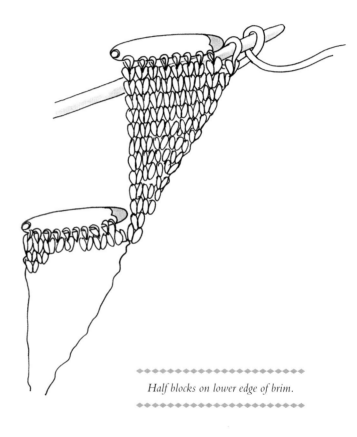

Half blocks on lower edge of brim.

BRIM With Color 1, knit first tier with 15 half blocks for lower edge of brim. Work back and forth following chart, using two dpn (U.S. 0 / 2 mm). The first block is shown on chart, Rows 1–20. Row 1 shows the cast-on with 2 sts.

After completing Row 20, place 10 sts on a safety pin. The last st + 1 backward loop CO will be the cast-on for the next half block.

Work Rows 21–40 14 times so that you have 15 half blocks, each one ending with 10 sts on a safety pin. On last half block, do not make a new backward loop after you have placed the last 10 sts on a holder. Cut yarn and draw end through rem st.

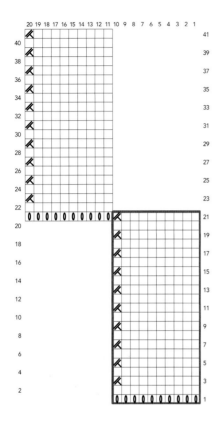

☐ knit on RS, purl on WS
⬈ join 1 st with 1 st from block to left with ssk
🛈 puk 1 st

Knit a tier of 15 whole blocks that lean left. Change to Color 2 and work each block back and forth, following chart. The repeat is framed in red.

Puk 10 sts along long side of a half block (= Row 1) and move the sts from the nearest block on the left side off the safety and onto a dpn.

At end of every RS row, join 1 st from new block together with 1 st from block below with ssk, until all sts from block below have been used up (= Row 21). Place the 10 sts from the new block on a safety pin and puk 10 new sts from the next block below. Row 21 of previous block will be Row 1 of new block.

Make a total of 15 left-leaning whole blocks.

Join brim into a circle by knitting the whole block picked up on the edge of the first half block with the sts from the last knitted half block. Make sure the band does not twist.

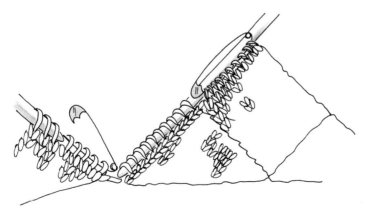

Whole blocks, leaning left, for middle of brim.

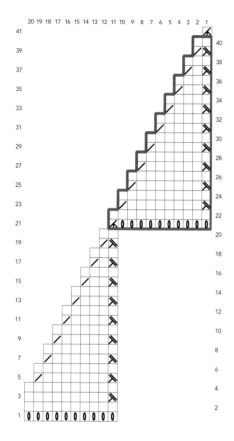

Half blocks for upper edge of brim.

☐ knit on RS, purl on WS
╱ k2tog
⋈ join 1 st with 1 st from block to right with p2tog
0 puk 1 st
⋏ p3tog on RS

Finish brim with a tier of half blocks that lean right. Change to Color 1 and work each half block back and forth, following chart. The repeat is framed in red.

Row 1 begins on WS, so that when blocks are worked to the right, stitches can be picked up on WS.

Pick up and work 10 sts along long side of previous block (= Row 1) and move the sts from the safety pin on the row below to a dpn (as for half blocks at beginning of brim).

At the beginning of every WS row, p2tog, and, at the end of the same row, p2tog with 1 st from new block + 1 st from block below until all sts from block below have been used (= Row 21). Pick up and work new sts from next block below. Row 21 will be Row 1 of new block.

Make a total of 15 right-leaning half blocks.

After completing last block, cut yarn and draw end through rem st.

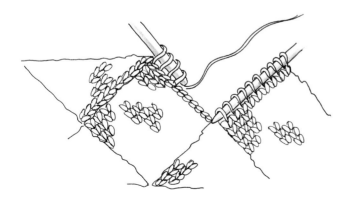

Half blocks, leaning right, for upper edge of brim.

SLIP STITCHES With Color 1, crochet 180 slip sts around each side of brim edges = 12 sts per block.

CENTER OF HAT With Color 1 and short circular, puk 180 sts in one of the slip stitch edges of the brim.

Join, pm for beg of rnd, and knit around in St st for 4¾ in / 12 cm. The rnd begins at center back.

NAME OR INITIALS Chart desired letters from alphabet on page 38 (Monogram). Find center of your pattern, and knit so that name/initials will be centered on hat.

Use Color 2 for name/initials, but do not carry yarn all the way around—that will make the hat draw in. Instead, cut yarn at end of each row of lettering. Ends will be hidden under the facing. Just be sure to leave about 1 in / 2 cm so that you can weave them into a couple of sts to keep them from peeping out later.

Continue working around in St st until hat is 8 in / 20 cm in stockinette as measured from slip stitch edge of brim.

HAT CROWN

Rnd 1: (K8, k2tog) around.

Rnds 2–6: Knit.

Rnd 7: (K7, k2tog) around.

Rnds 8–12: Knit.

Rnd 13: (K6, k2tog) around.

Rnds 14–18: Knit.

Rnd 19: (K5, k2tog) around.

Rnds 20–24: Knit.

Rnd 25: (K4, k2tog) around.

Change to dpn.

Rnds 26–30: Knit.

Rnd 31: (K3, k2tog) around.

Rnds 32–34: Knit. (Note that there are now only 3 rnds between decreases).

Rnd 35: (K2, k2tog) around.

Rnds 36–38: Knit.

Rnd 39: (K1, k2tog) around.

Rnds 40–42: Knit.

Rnd 43: K2tog around.

Rnd 44: Knit.

Cut yarn and draw end through rem 18 sts.

HAT LINING You can knit the lining for the hat with leftover yarn the same weight as the pattern yarn, just like the original Greta's hat. It's a good idea, however, to begin by knitting a few rounds with Color 1, since this section will be visible on RS when brim is folded up.

With Color 1, puk 180 sts in slip st edge of brim.

Tip: *Pm to mark beg of rnd.*

Knit around for 5½ in / 14 cm.

Make sure all ends are secured before you finish lining.

Work crown of lining as for outside of hat.

Fasten off the last end.

Wash hat in lukewarm water with wool-safe soap. Rinse if necessary. Roll in towel and then place over an inflated balloon (size equivalent to head of wearer) to dry.

Make pompom with Color 1 and sew securely to top of hat. For details, see "Tassels, pompoms, and I-cords" on page 13.

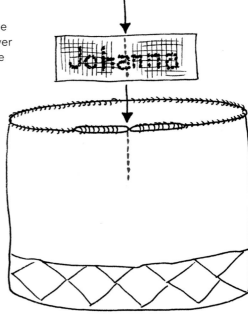

GRETA'S HAT
Original pattern

This hat is now part of Hermanna Stengård's collection, but it is not clear whether it was intended to be. One of Hermanna's granddaughters was named Greta; this could have been her hat, perhaps knitted by Grandmother Hermanna or by Greta herself.

The hat has a brim worked in entrelac with dark and light green yarn. The rest of the hat was continued from the brim with Greta's name and some flower motifs. The inside was knitted up from the edge and used all sorts of leftover yarn for a very fine striped lining inside the hat.

The hat is prettily striped with leftover yarn for the lining.

NORDIC KNITTING TRADITIONS

It's easy to see country borders on a map, but traditions and the exchange of goods and knowledge have never cared about nationality. Throughout history, knowledge about handcrafts has been spread through commerce and marriage, while boundaries have also shifted. So Nordic knitting traditions are wider-ranging than the Nordic countries as defined by maps.

Knitting came to England, Germany, and Holland before taking root in the Nordic countries. Iceland is thought to have been the first Nordic country where people knitted; knowledge of it came over the sea via merchants. Icelandic documents show that rents to the Bishop of Hólar were partially paid with knitted stockings at the end of the 1300s. Denmark's contact with Iceland is believed to be the reason why stocking knitting came to be practiced in Helsingör in the same time period.

In the Nordic countries, the technique of *nålbinding* (needle weaving) preceded knitting by several centuries. *Nålbinding* also used wool yarn to form fabric by connecting a series of loops.

Knitting's many advantages must have contributed to its rapid spread. No expensive work tools were necessary for knitting, and no materials went to waste. It was also easy to carry knitting along and many early sources describe women who knitted while going on long walks. Skilled hands should always be busy.

Towns with ports helped patterns spread. It's easy to tell which patterns have traditionally been used in any one village, but almost impossible to determine exactly where a motif was originally created. As patterns traveled through new towns and generations, they changed a little along the way and would be influenced by other textile techniques like weaving and embroidery. Regularly-fashioned motifs and diagonal patterns with distinct repeats across and lengthwise were easy to remember at a time when knowledge of mathematics wasn't very good.

Swedish has several names for the technique referred to in English as entrelac: *näverstickning*, *korgstickning*, and *pärtkorgsrutning*, all of which refer to birch bark or basket weaving techniques. The seemingly woven surface of entrelac consists of small knitted blocks. It's common in Nordic knitting, but we don't know exactly where it originally came from. However, we have early evidence of it in Norway and Finland, as well as on Gotland.

Today we have few knitted objects from before 1800. Everyday knitted garments were worn out over time and then ripped up when they could no longer be repaired, because the wool could be recarded and spun into new yarn for new garments. Wool has always been easy to recycle, and the fiber most used for knitting in Scandinavia was sheep's wool. Sheep were cheap to maintain and as long as the wool was sorted and prepared appropriately, it could be used for a wide variety of end products.

It's hard to pinpoint when knitting came to the Nordic countries for personal use, but much easier to document the trade in knitted goods, because a whole industry developed with traveling merchants. On Gotland, so-called "sweater hags" went to the mainland once a year with their own knitted garments and those they'd bought from others. By selling these goods, they gained an economic freedom which few women had in those times.

Bergen in Norway was a center for imports of various luxury goods, including knitted silk garments and wool garments. During the 1600s, a knitting school was established for girls—which helped knitting spread throughout Norway.

The Norwegian army needed a huge number of stockings, which also became an important trade item around the Baltic Sea. Stockings were the first garments that were knitted in large numbers, and that has influenced knitting terminology. Today Scandinavians refer to double-pointed needles as "stocking needles," even though they are also used to knit mittens, sleeves, and hats. The word "stockings" has also influenced the name of the "smooth" stitch used for stocking knitting: "stockinette" in American English or "stocking stitch" in British terminology.

On Gotland, a bride-to-be needed to have at least a dozen pairs of handknitted stockings in her hope chest. In Finland, the tradition went even further back, and a Finnish bride was expected to have enough stockings to last 20 years.

Decorative patterning on stockings was often placed around the gusset between the foot, heel, and leg. The Scandinavian *vadmal* and fulled knitting are basically the same in principle: A woven or knitted surface is felted so hard that it becomes rigid, holding warmth in and moisture out. The resulting durability is considerable when compared with the original woven or knitted fabric. Yarn for stockings needed to be very strong to tolerate wear from shoes. Stocking yarn was spun with more twists in the singles and plied harder than other yarn. Sometimes sheep's wool was blended with linen, mohair, goat hair, cow hair, horsehair, or human hair to make it stronger.

In the cold climate of the Nordic countries, mittens have always been necessary outside during the winter. When it was especially cold, people might wear two pairs of mittens, one over the other, or wear a pair of knitted mittens inside leather mittens. Protective knitted wool wrist warmers could be worn over any gap at the wrist. Mittens for anyone who worked in the forest had completely different functional requirements than mittens used by fishermen. In Bohus, on the west coast of Sweden, each mitten was often knitted with two thumbs so the wearer could turn them when one side became wet or torn at the thumbhole.

According to Norwegian traditions from Selbu, Telemark, and Gudbrandsdalen, a bride should knit especially fine mittens for the bridegroom, his father, all his brothers, and everyone in the bridal party. That meant a lot of mittens, and many of these are still preserved today in museums.

Up until 1900, only men wore hats. Women wore shawls that they could wrap around their heads. In Norway, the hat was often part of simpler local folk costumes. Machine-knitted red hats became particularly popular. During the 1780s, red hats were one of the items made at the Norwegian Unity Factory, which also sold hats in Sweden. Even in Finland, red hats were popular, but with a cone-shaped or rounded crown. The most common hats were doubled and reversible, or single layer, with or without a folded-up brim. In west Finland, men's costumes often included a pointed "stocking" cap. Even in Denmark, a red hat called a "night cap" was worn daily by peasant men. *Nikulør* hats were Danish hats patterned with many colors, worn by farmers south of Fyn. These were doubled hats with knitted linings folded into the outer shell. Hats were also knitted as engagement presents. At the end of the nineteenth century, smoking hats were popular, preferably with a long pointy top that ended with a tassel on a cord—the longer the better.

Wool was mostly used in natural colors, but white wool was especially desirable because it could be dyed for fine clothing. Yellows could be derived from birch leaves, golden marguerite (*Anthemis tinctoria*), and tansy. Sometimes alum was added for a clearer yellow color. Juniper twigs and oak bark made gray; some mosses yielded red brown if the yarn was mordanted with iron. Black came from brazilwood and overdyed dark gray wool. Blue was obtained with indigo purchased from India, but a slightly more gray-blue shade

could be extracted from woad (*Isatis tinctoria*). Green shades were obtained by first dyeing the yarn yellow and then dipping it in indigo.

There are also indications that bedstraw or woodruff, a relative of madder, was grown in Nordic regions and used to yield some red shades. Brighter reds needed to be bought, and were very much in demand. After 1870, the first synthetic aniline dyes became very popular commercially because of their bright colors.

Wool contains lanolin, a fat that makes the fibers easier to spin. People thought that knitting garments with unwashed yarn made them softer when they were later washed after finishing. Lanolin also made it easier to full or felt wool so the garment became more durable.

Today we often wear out wool clothes by washing them too much. People used to wash woolens rarely. Some stains might be washed out, but often garments were simply hung outside to air. Wool stays cleaner by airing out: Not only bad smells but even particles of dirt disappear. This is because of the way wool resists dampness. When the humidity of the air is high, the protein molecules in the wool fiber absorb the moisture. When the outside humidity is low, the moisture is drawn back out—and little particles of dirt come out with it.

Today many people associate Nordic knitting patterns with sweaters, particularly Icelandic Lopi sweaters, which became popular in the 1950s. These sweaters were actually an experiment in the 1920s; people wanted to see whether they could knit with unspun pencil roving. The Norwegian lice sweater is also well-known, and was originally knitted only in black and white. The name "lice sweater" is derived from the original pattern's appearance, black dots on a white background.

BIBLIOGRAPHY

Bergdahl, Violet and Ella Skoglund. *Gotländsk sticksöm* [Gotland Knitting]. Stockholm, Sweden: LTs förlag, 1983.

Bjelland, Anna Marøt, et al. *Votter og vantar* [Mittens and Gloves]. Oslo, Norway: Aschehoug, 1955.

Bondesen, Esther. *Den nya stickboken* [The New Knitting Book]. Stockholm, Sweden: Lindqvists, 1945.

Christoffersson, Britt-Marie. *Swedish Sweaters: New Designs from Historical Examples.* Newtown, CT: Taunton, 1990.

Feitelson, Ann. *The Art of Fair Isle Knitting: History, Technique, Color and Patterns.* Loveland, Colorado, 1996.

Fredholm, Inger. *Stickning.* [Knitting]. Stockholm, Sweden: Wahlström & Widstrand, 1978.

Gottfridsson, Inger and Ingrid Gottfridsson. *The Swedish Mitten Book: Traditional Patterns from Gotland.* Asheville, NC: Lark, 1984.

Gustafsson, Kerstin and Alan Waller. *Ull: hemligheter, möjligheter, färdigheter* [Wool: Secrets, Possibilities, Preparations]. Stockholm, Sweden: LTs förlag, 1987.

Hazelius Berg, Gunnel, et al. *Stickat och virkat i nordisk tradition* [Knitting and Crochet in the Nordic Tradition]. Vasa, Finland: Österbottens Museum.1984.

Hedemann, Ellinor and Harriet Clayhills. *Lus, stjärnor och timglas: Vi sticker gamla nordiska mönster på vår tids vis* [Lice, Stars, and Hourglasses: Knitting old Nordic motifs in our contemporary way]. Stockholm, Sweden: Prisma, 1978.

Johansson, Britta and Kersti Nilsson. *Binge—a halländsk sticktradition* [Binge—a Halland Knitting Tradition]. Stockholm: LTs förlag, 1980.

Lind, Vibeke. *Knitting in the Nordic Tradition.* Asheville, NC: Lark, 1984.

Lund Jensen, Aase and Karen Lind Petersen. *Moderne strik efter danske almuemønstre* [Modern Knitting inspired by Danish peasant patterns]. Copenhagen, Denmark: Høst og Søn,1959.

McGregor, Sheila. *The Complete Book of Traditional Scandinavian Knitting.* New York: St. Martin's, 1984, reprinted 2004.

Mucklestone, Mary Jane. *150 Scandinavian Designs.* Loveland, CO: Interweave, 2013.

Pagoldh, Susanne. *Nordic Knitting: Thirty-One Patterns in the Scandinavian Tradition.* Loveland, CO: Interweave, 1987.

Paradis Gustafsson, Kerstin. *Ull och ull tekniker* [Wool and Wool Techniques]. GML fölag (on-demand printing): 2013.

Pettersson-Berg, Anna. *Mönsterstickning* [Pattern Knitting]. 1924.

Ploug, Marianne. *Gamle Lollandkse strikkemønstre* [Old Lolland knitting motifs]. Maribo, Denmark: Museum Maribo, 1981.

Rowe, Mary. *Knitted Tams.* Loveland, Colorado: Interweave, 1989.

Sibbern Böhn, Annichen. *Norwegian Knitting Designs.* Seattle, WA: Spinningwheel, 2011 [original Norwegian edition published in 1929].

Snidare, Uuve. *Fiskartröjor och anda tröjklassiker* [Fishermen's Sweaters and Other Classic Sweaters]. Stockholm, Sweden: Prisma1986.